FISH PACKAGING TECHNOLOGY

About the Editor

Dr. K. Gopakumar is currently the Director of the Central Institute of Fisheries Technology (Indian Council of Agricultural Research) at Cochin, India. An authority on handling, processing and preservation of tropical fish, Dr. Gopakumar took his Masters Degree in Chemistry and later Ph.D. in Biochemistry form the University of Kerala. As the Head of the Fish Processing Technology Division of the Central Institute of Fisheries Technology, he played a crucial role in modernising the fish processing industry in India. He has authored more than 125 research publications in various international journals.

Dr. Gopakumar has travelled extensively and has chaired many international conferences on fish processing technology. He is currently the working party member of the Indo Pacific Commission on Fish Technology and Marketing (FAO), member of the Committee III/9 of the International Union of Nutrition Sciences, Chairman of the Sectional Committee FADC 12 for Fish and Fisheries Products of the Bureau of Indian Standards and Editorial Consultant of the *Fish Tech News* published by FAO. Recently he was elected as the President of the Society of Fishery Technologists (India). Dr. Gopakumar has contributed status and review papers to several internationally acclaimed books on fishery technology and also is a member of all national bodies connected with fish processing and laying down standards for Indian Fishery Products.

FISH PACKAGING TECHNOLOGY

Materials and Methods

Edited by

K. GOPAKUMAR

Director

Central Institute of Fisheries Technology

Cochin-682 029, Kerala, India

Foreword by

PROF. P.V. DEHADRAI

Dy. Director General (Fy.)

Indian Council of Agricultural Research

Krishi Bhavan, New Delhi-110 001, India

CONCEPT PUBLISHING COMPANY PVT. LTD.

NEW DELHI-110059

ISBN: 978-81-7022-452-5

First Published 1993

Published and Printed by

Concept Since 1974

Concept Publishing Company Pvt. Ltd.
A/15-16, Commercial Block, Mohan Garden,
New Delhi-110059 (India)
T : 91-11-41101460
E : publishing@conceptpub.com, *W*: www.conceptpub.com

FOREWORD

Packaging is known to have brought out a revolution in the marketing and distribution of food and food products in the world. Improved methods of packaging have helped not only in keeping food safe with longer shelf-life but also helped in enhancing its consumer acceptance.

From among the perishable materials, fish is the most sensitive commodity and is prone to quick degradation even when kept under chilled or frozen storage. Fish transport, distribution and market is unfortunately at the lowest technical standard in India and this is so particularly in the domestic marketing sector.

About 25–30 per cent of the fish landed in India is used for dried fish production. Due to lack of adequate storage and packaging methodology, the dried fish losses are often as high as 30–40 per cent. Packaging and storage methods for dried fish products is all the more important when the commodity is to be sold/distributed in rural areas. The present publication describes certain important methods of packaging dried fish.

The value added fish products such as quick frozen fish, frozen shrimp etc. are being processed for super markets in the developed countries of European and American continent. It is essential to meet the standards of packaging while promoting the Indian products in such sophisticated markets. In fact, the future of the domestic and export market for fish and fish products would largely be influenced by the development of packaging technology in India.

The present publication is first ever compilation of its kind, written and edited on the subject of packaging for fish. The book describes several aspects of packaging for different types of fishery products. The contributions have been drawn selectively from authors who are proven leaders in their fields of specialisations.

The present volume would be of immense use not only to the entrepreneurs in fishery industry but also to those who are associated with the science of packaging.

Indian Council of Agricultural Research
Krishi Bhavan, New Delhi 110001

Prof. P.V. DEHADRAI
Dy. Director General (Fy.)

August 1, 1991

PREFACE

Modern materials used for packaging have revolutionized food industries. A processed food item has an optimum shelf-life under different conditions of storage. A good packaging never improves quality of product but it can prevent deterioration to some extent. Packaging can considerably enhance consumer acceptability and thereby enhance saleability of product. Modern seafood industries need a variety of packaging materials requiring different quality standards.

One of the important problems faced by Indian seafood industry is the non-availability of quality packagings for their use compared to their counterparts elsewhere in the world. This often results in poor acceptability of their products in the markets of western world. It also restricts their entry into super markets of Europe and U.S.A. There have been several requests from my friends, seafood technologists and processors, to bring out a publication giving some background information on packaging materials and methods for their use. This book represents a collection of articles edited by me with a view to catering this long felt need of Indian Seafood Industry.

The articles in this book are written by selected experts in the field. They cover a wide spectrum of methods, materials and processes currently in use for seafood processing. They are equally applicable to all food industries in general.

I am grateful to Dr. P.V.Dehadrai, Deputy Director General (Fisheries Division) of the Indian Council of Agricultural Research for writing a fitting foreword to this book. Several senior scientists of the Central Institute of Fisheries Technology have given me valuable suggestions in the shaping of the book. The most notable among them are my colleagues in the Processing Division, M/s. T.K. Srinivasa Gopal and S.K. Bhattacharyya. The technical assistance given by Mr. V.K. Ibrahim for drawing and typing work done by Ms N. Leena and Mr. K.V. Mathai are gratefully acknowledged.

K. GOPAKUMAR

CONTENTS

LIST OF CONTRIBUTORS

K.P. Antony
Scientist, Central Institute of Fisheries Technology, Cochin-682029.

K.K. Balachandran
Principal Scientist, Division of Fish Processing, Central Institute of Fisheries Technology, Cochin-682029.

S.K. Bhattacharyya
Scientist, Central Institute of Fisheries Technology, Cochin-682029.

M/s Caprihans (India) Ltd. Bombay

Joseph Francis
Professor, Department of Polymer Science and Rubber Technology, Cochin University of Science and Technology, Cochin-682022.

N.X. George
Managing Director, Super Packaging Industries, Cochin-688534.

K. Gopakumar
Director, Central Institute of Fisheries Technology, Cochin-682029.

K.R. Kumar
Senior Scientist, Centre for Food Packaging, Central Food Technological Research Institute, Mysore-570013.

R.A.N. Murthy
Centre for Food Packaging, Central Food Technological Research Institute, Mysore-570013.

P.G.K. Nair
Optima Packagings Limited, Cochin-682020.

T.K. Parameswaran
Production Manager, Travancore Rayons, Kerala.

P.A. Perigreen
Scientist, Central Institute of Fisheries Technology, Cochin-682029.

P.V. Prabhu
Principal Scientist, Central Institute of Fisheries Technology, Cochin-682029.

R.S. Ramasubramanian
Optima Packagings Limited, Cochin-682020.

C.V.N. Rao
Principal Scientist, Central Institute of Fisheries Technology, Cochin-682029.

T.K. Srinivasa Gopal
Scientist, Central Institute of Fisheries Technology, Cochin-682029.

K.K. Talwar
Managing Director, Paper Products Ltd. Bombay.

LIST OF TABLES

LIST OF FIGURES

LIST OF ABBREVIATIONS

ABS	-	Acrylonitrile butadiene styrene
ASTM	-	American Society for testing materials
BA	-	Barrier layer
BONylon	-	Biaxially oriented nylon
BO PET	-	Biaxially oriented polyester
BOPP	-	Biaxially oriented polypropylene
BIS	-	Bureau of Indian Standards
BPF	-	British Plastic Federation
BSI	-	British Standards Institution
CFB	-	Corrugated fibre board
CFTRI	-	Central Food Technological Research Institute
CIFT	-	Central Institute of Fisheries Technology
CPP	-	Cast polypropylene
EEA	-	Ethylene ethyl acrylate
EEC	-	European Economic Community
ERH	-	Equilibrium relative humidity
EVA	-	Ethylene-vinyl acetate copolymer
EVAL/EVOH	-	Ethylene-vinyl alcohol
FDA	-	Food and Drug Administration, USA
HDPE	-	High density polyethylene
HM-HDPE	-	High molecular-High density polyethylene
HV	-	Bonding agent
EAA	-	Ethylene acrylic acid copolymer
ISI	-	Indian Standards Institution
ISO	-	International Standards Organisation
LDPE	-	Low-density polyethylene
LLDPE	-	Linear low-density polyethylene
MA	-	Modified atmosphere
MLF	-	Multi-layer film
MPEDA	-	Marine Products Export Development Authority

MSAT	- Moisture proof, Heat sealable, Anchored transparent film
MST (cellophane)	- Moisture proof, heat sealable transparent film
MXXT	- Moisture proof, PVDC coated on both sides transparent film
OECD	- Organisation for Economic Co-operation and Development
OTR	- Oxygen transmission rate
PA	- Polyamide
PAN	- Polyacrylo nitrile
PC	- Polycarbonate
PE	- Polyethylene (Polythene)
PET	- Polyethylene tetra phthalate (Polyester)
PETP	- Polyethylene tetra phthalate (Polyester)
PP	- Polypropylene
ppm	- Parts per million
PS	- Polystyrene
PT (cellophane)	- Plain transparent cellophane
PVC	- Polyvinylchloride
PVDC	- Polyvinylidenechloride
QSAT	- Opaque heat sealable anchored transparent film
RH	- Relative humidity
WVTR	- Water vapour transmission rate

ONE

PLASTIC FILMS: MANUFACTURING METHODS

JOSEPH FRANCIS

I. EXTRUSION OF FILM

There are fundamentally two different methods of extruding film, namely, blow extrusion and slit die extrusion. The equipment for film extrusion consists of an extruder, fitted with a suitable die, equipment to cool the molten film, haul-off machinery and a wind-up unit. Blow extrusion and slit die extrusion vary in the design of die used and in the type of cooling. The haul-off and wind-up equipment is also different.

The basic extrusion process is designed to convert continously, a thermoplastics material into a film.

A typical extruder is shown in Fig. 1.1 and consists essentially of an Arcimedean screw which revolves within a close fitting, heated barrel. The plastic granules are fed through a hopper mounted at one end of the barrel and carried forward along the barrel by the action of the screw. As the granules move along the screw, they are melted by contact with the heated walls of the barrel and by the heat generated by friction. The screw then forces the molten plastic through the die which determines its final form. The most important component of the extruder is the screw and different designs of screw are used for extruding different polymers. Extruder screws are characterised by their length to diameter ratio (commonly written as L/D ratio) and their compression ratios. The compression ratio is the ratio of the volume of one flight of the screw at the hopper end to the volume of one flight at the die end. L/D ratios most commonly used for single screw extruders are between 15:1 to 30:1 while

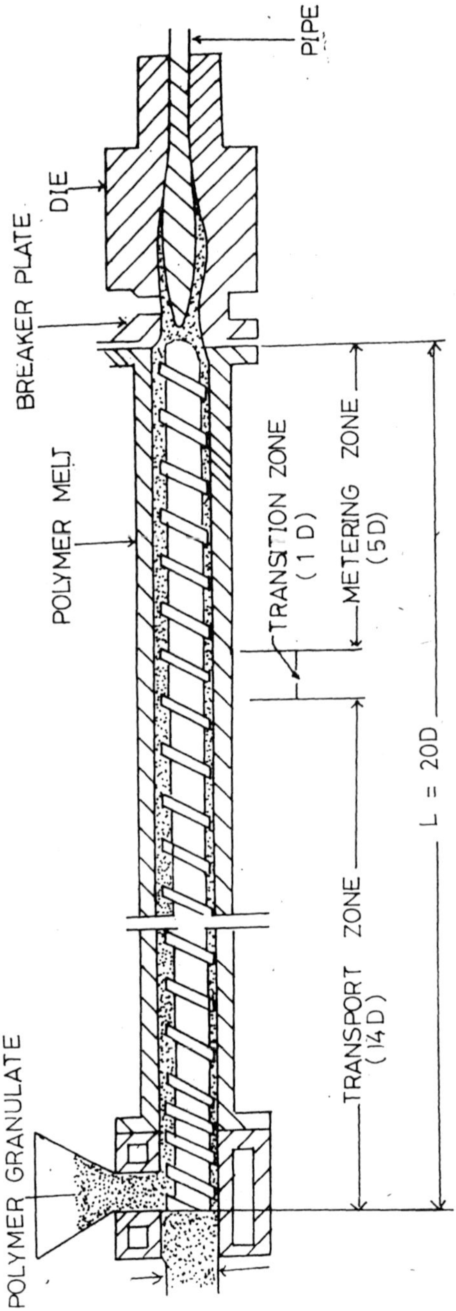

FIG. 1.1: Scheme for a typical single screw extruder (L/D = 20) shown extruding pipe

compression ratios can vary from 2:1 to 4:1. An extruder screw is usually divided into three sectors, namely, feed, compression and metering. The feed section transports the material from the hopper mouth to the hotter portion of the barrel. The compression section is that section where the diminishing depth of thread causes a volume compression of the melting granules. The main effect of this is an increase in the shearing action on the molten polymer due to the relative motion of the screw surface with respect to the barrel wall. This improves the mixing and also leads to an increase in frictional heat and a more uniform heat distribution throughout the melt. The function of the final section of the screw is to homogenise the melt further, meter it uniformly through the die and smooth out pulsations.

Just prior to the die, is fitted a breaker plate supporting a screen pack consisting of a number of fine or coarse mesh gauges. The screen pack filters out any contamination which might be present in the raw material. This is particularly important in the case of thin film extrusion where even the smallest of contaminating particles could cause holes or even breaks in the film. The screen pack also increases the back pressure in the extruder and this improves the mixing and homogenisation of the melt.

Blown Film Extrusion

A typical set-up for blown film extrusion is shown in Fig. 1.2. In this instance the molten polymer from the extruder enters the die from the side but entry can also be effected from the bottom of the die. Once in the die, the molten polymer is made to flow round a mandrel and emerges through a ring shaped die opening, in the form of a tube. The tube is expanded into a bubble of the required diameter by an air pressure maintained through the centre of the mandrel. The expansion of the bubble is accompanied by a corresponding reduction in thickness. Extrusion of the tube is usually upwards but it can be extruded downwards, or even sideways. The bubble pressure is maintained by pinch rolls at one end and by the die at the other. It is important that the pressure of the air is kept constant in order to ensure uniform thickness and width of film. Other factors that affect film thickness are extruder output, haul-off speed and temperatures of the die and along the barrel. These must also be strictly controlled.

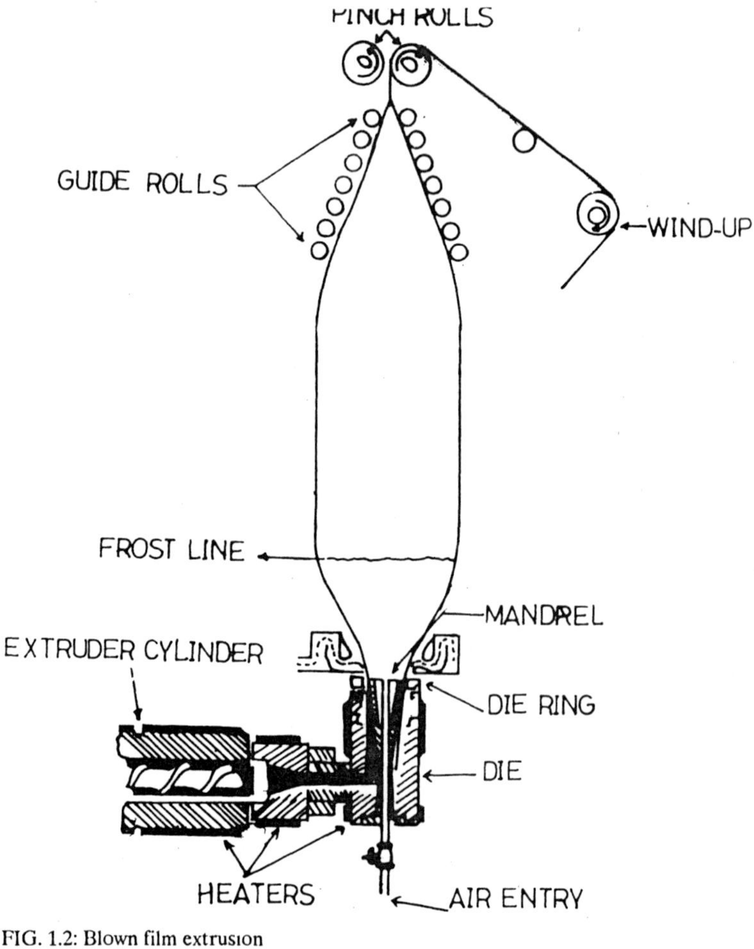

FIG. 1.2: Blown film extrusion

Slit-die Extrusion (Flat Film Extrusion)

In flat film extrusion the molten polymer is extruded through a slit-die and thence into a quenching water bath or on to a chilled roller. In either case the essence of the process is rapid cooling of the extruded film and cooling is, therefore, applied within a very short distance of the die lips (usually between 25 and 65 mm). This short distance is also dictated by the necessity to reduce 'neckling' of the film web, with consequent loss of width. In the chill roll casting method, the melt is extruded on to a chromium plated roller, cored for water cooling. The rapid cooling leads to the formation of small crystallites and this gives a clearer film.

Where the quench bath method is used, the water temperature should be kept constant for best results. At constant extrusion temperature, lower quench temperatures improve slip and anti-blocking properties while higher quench temperatures give film that is easier to wind without wrinkles and with better physical properties.

Comparison of Blow and Cast Film Process

Some of the advantages of the tubular film process are as follows:

1. The mechanical properties of the film are generally better than those of cast film.
2. The width of lay flat film is easily adjustable and there are no losses due to edge trimming. This latter is necessary for flat film because of the thickening of the film edge due to necking in.
3. Lay flat film is more easily converted into bags since it is only necessary to seal one end of a cut length to make the bag.
4. The cost for making wide blown film is much lower than for wide cast film because the cost of chill rollers increases rapidly with width due to the difficulty of precision grinding in longer rollers.
5. A tubular film die is more compact and is cheaper than a slit-die producing film of comparable width.
6. The tubular process is easier and more flexible to operate.

These advantages must be balanced against the advantages of the slit-die process which are as follows:

1. Very high outputs can be obtained by slit-die extrusion units.
2. Slit-die film normally has superior optical properties but it should be noted that special rapid cooling processes have been developed for tubular film, particularly in the case of polypropylene film. One example, the Shell Tubular Quench Process, will be described in more detail later.

3. Thickness variation is usually less with slit-die extruded film.

II. CALENDERING

Calendering is a process for producing film or sheet by feeding a plastic mass into the nip between two rolls where it is squeezed into a film which then passes round other rolls. It emerges as a continuous film, the thickness of which is governed by the gap between the last pair of rolls.

The first stage of a calendering process is the compounding of the plastics mix fed to the calender rolls. Where polyethylene is being calendered, the mix may be a simple hot melt but in the case of PVC (which is the polymer most commonly converted by calendering) the procedure is more complex. One method is to pre-mix the polymer in a ribbon blender with stabilizers, plasticizers, etc., and then pass the blend to an internal mixer where the mass is gelled for about 5-10 min at about 120-160°C. The gelated lumps so formed are made into a rough sheet on a two-roll mill and the sheet fed to the calender.

Calenders may consist of from two to five hollow rolls (or bowls) arranged for steam heating or water cooling and are characterised by the number of bowls and their arrangement as for example, I, Z or inverted L types. Four rolls, inverted L and Z types are the most usual.

Calendering usually produces film with a better uniformity of gauge compared with that obtained by extrusion. A number of factors contribute to this, one of which is the great care paid to the engineering of the calender bowls (as mentioned earlier). The final gauge is very much dependant on the gap between the final two bowls whereas in extrusion, the gauge is dependant more on blow-up ratios (in the case of tubular film) or draw down speeds (in the case of slit-die film). In addition, in an extruder cross-head die there may be a range of path lengths which lead to preferential flow and induce variation in gauge. In the tubular die process there are complicating factors such as the structures supporting the mandrel in the die. This also has an effect on the melt flow, leading to gauge variations.

Another advantage of calendering is that better mixing is obtained. The amount of energy available in a calendering line is very much more than in an extrusion line, so calendered film is less dependant on the uniformity of the feedstock.

The main advantage of extrusion for PVC is the much lower

capital costs involved, so that shorter runs can be made at economic rates.

III. SOLVENT CASTING

Solvent casting methods are expensive but cellulose nitrate film was made in this way because of the flammable nature of the film. A casting solution is prepared by dissolving cellulose nitrate and camphor (as plasticizer) in a 70:30 ether/alcohol mixture using paddle mixers. After 8-10 hrs mixing the product is filtered through cellulose wadding and de-aerated in vacuum at a temperature just under the boiling point of the solvent.

The film casting is carried out on an endless belt, a smooth surface being obtained by depositing a layer of hard gelatin on a copper support. After being stripped from the casting surface the film is seasoned in a heated drying cabinet where it passes over a zig zag pattern of rollers. After a final passage over chilled rollers to cool the film, it is wound into reels. The general lay-out of a film casting process is shown in Fig. 1.3.

Some cellulose acetate film is produced by solvent casting, as well as by extrusion, and solution casting has also been used for producing vinyl chloride/vinyl acetate copolymer films.

Casting of Regenerated Cellulose Film

The basic raw material, cellulose, is obtained from wood pulp or cotton linters. After soaking in caustic soda for an hour, the excess alkali is pressed out. It is then shredded and allowed to age for 2-3 days and absorbs oxygen from the air. This reduces the length of the cellulose molecule chain and so reduces the viscosity of the solution during the next stage. Here the pulp is transferred to rotating churns and then sprayed with carbon disulphide. The solution is discharged into a tank and dispersed by stirring with dilute caustic soda solution. The resultant solution is known as viscose.

Cellulose film is made by filtering the viscose solution and allowing it to 'ripen' for 4-5 days. The ripening process consists of a slow hydrolysis, the progress of which is followed by taking viscocisty measurements. If ripening goes too far, a gel is formed which is useless. Air bubbles in the solution are removed by drawing a vacuum and a film is formed by casting on to a drum of endless metal

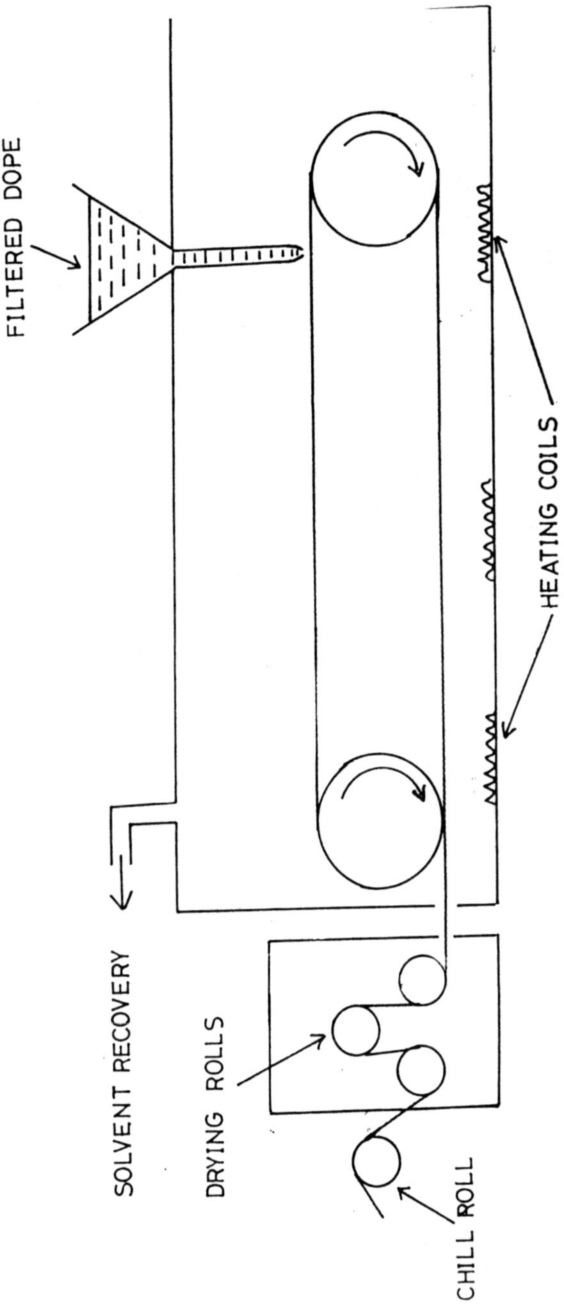
FILTERED DOPE
HEATING COILS
SOLVENT RECOVERY
DRYING ROLLS
CHILL ROLL

band, which revolves in the first of a series of tanks. The thickness of the film is regulated by varying the orifice at the base of the casting hopper or reservoir.

The first tank contains the coagulating solution consisting of sulphuric acid and sodium sulphate at a temperature of about 40°C. This solution not only coagulates the viscose but initiates its regeneration back to cellulose. The coagulated film is then led through further tanks by means of guide rolls. The tanks contain various solutions designed to complete the regeneration, wash out acid carried over from the coagulating bath, remove any elemental sulphur, carbon disulphide, hydrogen sulphide, etc. and bleach the now transparent but still slightly coloured film. The film is then run through a bath containing glycerol or ethylene glycol which act as plasticizers and confer flexibility on the film. Finally it is passed through a drying oven and reeled up.

At this stage, the film is extremely permeable to moisture vapour and is not heat sealable and a subsequent coating teatment must be given if moistureproofness or heat sealability are required. A typical coating consists of dibutyl phthalate-plasticised cellulose nitrate, together with waxes and natural resins dissolved in organic solvents. Urea formaldehyde is also incorporated to anchor the coating and prevent it from floating off in damp conditions. The film is passed through the coating bath, dried to evaporate the solvent, then passed through a high humidity chamber to restore the flexibility. Where even better barrier properties are required, a coating of polyvinylidene chloride is applied.

REFERENCES

Briston, J.H., 1983: *Plastic Films*, George Gordwin (Longman Group Ltd.).
Oswin, C.R., 1975: *Plastic Films and Packaging*, Applied Science Publishers, London.

TWO

CELLOPHANE

T.K. PARAMESHWARAN

Cellulosic polymers are derived from natural cellulose which is a main substance of all plants. Cellulose is composed of anhydroglucose (glucose has a molecular formula $C_6H_{12}O_6$ and anhydroglucose $C_6H_{10}O_5$). In the natural cellulose, number of glucose units vary from 3000 to 4000. The structure shows 3 hydroxyl groups on each glucose unit. The presence of numerous polar -OH groups and high molecular weight results in very strong rigidity and crystallinity to the polymer resulting in high softening point and insolubility. To make the cellulose more amenable for manufacturing purposes, it is necessary to decrease these intermolecular forces by reducing the molecular weight and/or by neutralizing the polar characters of the -OH groups.

I. HISTORICAL BACKGROUND

In the year 1892, two English Scientists C.F. Gross and E.J. Bevan found that a suitable derivative of cellulose can be obtained by reacting it with alkali and carbon disulphide, which can later be dissolved easily in dilute alkali to give indirectly a solution of cellulose and this reaction famously known as "viscose" reaction paved the way later for the manufacture of cellulose film. Since then several attempts have been made to regenerate the cellulose as a film and various have been issued, notable amongst them being the one by C.H. Stearn of England in 1898. The credit for making continuous film from viscose goes to the Swiss German Scientist Dr. Branden Berger who, in the year 1906 invented the process for making regenerated cellulose film in a continuous sheet form. Till 1912 various experiments were done to perfect this product and to make it suitable for packaging purposes and in the year 1913 the firm S.A. La cellophane was established in Paris for commercial production of cellulose film. Although this film was in commercial production since 1913, it was only in the year 1927 that M/s. W.H. Charch and K.E. Pindle of USA found out that by application of a water-proof coating, this film can be made moisture proof. Since then many different grades of coated film have been made having in view of specific properties and requirements.

II. CLASSIFICATION

Cellulosic films

- Regenerated cellulose of cellulose hydrate
  - Viscose film (Cellophane)
  - Cuprammonium film
- Derivatives of cellulose
  - Cellulose acetate film
  - Cellulose nitrate film

Regenerated Cellulose

This is essentially same as natural cellulose, but has a lower molecular weight, containing only 300 to 500 glucose units. This lower molecular weight decreases greatly the intermolecular forces between the individual chains, thereby making it possible to obtain cellulose in a solution form. The reduction in molecular weight is accomplished by special chemical treatments such as viscose process, the cellulose pulp is treated with NaOH solution when sodium cellulose is formed. It is then exposed to CS_2 vapours (Xanthation) and the resulting yellow compound is dissolved in dilute caustic soda to give a solution i.e. viscose. From this, cellulose can be regenerated by neutralising the caustic soda with H_2SO_4.

III. MANUFACTURE

A. Raw Materials

(i) High purity wood pulp

(ii) High purity caustic soda
(iii) Sulphuric acid
(iv) Carbon di-sulfide
(v) Sodium sulphate
(vi) Sodium sulphide
(vii) Bleach liquor
(viii) Antichlor material
(ix) Glycerine/Plasticizers
(x) Surface active agents
(xi) Surface coating materials
(xii) Solvents
(xiii) Dyes and pigments

B. Process

Steeping

In this process the pulp in the form of sheets are steeped in an upright position, in strong caustic soda solution (17-20%) in specially designed hydraulic presses, called steeping presses. The pulp absorbs caustic soda, swells up considerably and the cellulose gets converted to alkali cellulose. Subsequently the sheets are pressed at a very great pressure to squeeze out the excess caustic soda.

Shredding and Maturing

The alkali cellulose sheets discharged from the steeping presses are fed into specially shaped shredding machines, where coating discs with spikes break the sheets and reduce them to a fluffy powder called alkali cellulose crumbs to density 150-200 g per litre. This alkali cellulose contain 15-16% sodium hydroxide, 30-36% cellulose and the rest water. These are then fed into a long gaint drum rotating at a slow speed and fitted with a small gradient.

The alkali cellulose is fed at one end and it slowly moves forward and is taken out at the other end. 12-24 hours elapse within this period. The whole drum is having a jacket in which water at constant temperature is circulated. During this period the cellulose molecules undergo certain controlled degradation is termed "aging or maturing". In the process of aging oxygen is absorbed and the length of the cellulose chain is shortened.

Xanthating and Dissolving

The matured alkali cellulose crumbs are then treated with liquid carbon di-sulphide in specially made rotating churns wherein they get converted into an orange coloured mass called cellulose xanthate. Initially the reaction takes place at a temperature of about 20°C which is permitted to raise to about 30°C towards the end of the cycle. After the reaction is completed dilute caustic soda solution is added and the xanthate is dissolved in it to give a honey like thick liquid called viscose (this liquid contains 7 to 8% cellulose and 5 to 6% caustic soda).

The chemical reactions involved in the preparation of viscose may be represented by the equations

$$ROH + NaOH \quad RONA + H_2O$$
$$RONa + CS_2 \quad RO\text{-}CS\text{-}SNa$$

Where R represents the cellulose molecule.

Ripening

Viscose solution is then ripened by keeping it for a period of 20-40 hours under low temperature is separate tanks. During this period of ripening, the viscose solution is filtered 2 or 3 times to remove all impurities and also exposed to high vacuum to remove all trapped air bubbles.

Casting and Washing

After proper ripening, filtration and deaeration, the viscose solution is pumped by a special metering pump into an extruder hopper. Viscose solution is cast in the form of a sheet in this hopper. Viscose solution is cast in the form of a sheet in this hopper which has two highly polished nickel alloy lips at the lower part. The tips of these lips are kept immersed in a solution containing sulphuric acid and sodium sulphate and as soon as viscose solution comes out of the hopper it meets the acid bath and gets coagulated into a solid sheet. This sheet is then fed through a series of tanks fitted with rollers and glass guides and containing various treatments baths for washing, sulphur removal, bleaching, again washing and plasticising. After this washing and purifying of the film, it is guided through the drying section, where with the help of hot air and steam heated rollers film is dried and wound in the form of rolls. The film produced thus is a plain transparent sheeting. The properties familiar and most useful to the customer, converter and end user viz. moisture proofness, heat sealability, freedom from blocking etc. are built in the film by application of specialised surface coatings.

IV. STORAGE – HANDLING

35-45 per cent RH, 18-24°C, Direct exposure to sunlight and extreme temperature should be avoided; film rolls not to be dropped/ dumped. Always kept in moisture barrier materials. Should be held horizontally by the core at each end.

V. CONVERSION

Methods and forms:	Coating
	Lamination
	Printing
	Conversion to bags, pouches, tapes, etc.
Coating:	Wax/hot melts
	Dispersion coating
	Nitrocellulose lacquer
	Polymers/co-polymers
Lamination:	Dry, heat, wax and wet lamination
Printing:	Flexography and gravure
Metallising:	With aluminium foil/high vacuum process

VI. FILM TYPES

This is done by letter designation:

A – Anchored
C – Coloured
D – Demi (one side) coated
H – Resistant to Blocking in humid atmosphere
J – Flame resistance
L – Less moisture proof than standard
M – Moisture proof

O – Opaque
P – Plain
R – Rancidity retardant
S – Heat sealing
T – Transparent
U – Unsized, low surface slippage
XX – Polymer coated

Gauges:
Normal – 300, 400 and 600
(Indicates weight of 10 sq.metres of film)

Type	Substance (gm/m^2)
300 gauge plain	27-34
300 gauge coated	32-37
400 gauge plain	38-45
400 gauge coated	40-47
600 gauge plain	56-64
600 gauge coated	60-68

VII. APPLICATIONS

Wraps

Food
Cigarettes
Toilet, *Agarbatti* and Cosmetics
Pharmaceuticals
Engineering, Rubber
Liquor
Fireworks
Textiles

Twist-wrap

Confectionery

Bags/Pouches

Dry fish, tea, coffee and other foods
Textiles, Hosiery

Base/Release Agent

Cello-tape
Fibreglass laminates

Tear off tapes and ribbons Strip packing – pharmaceutical

VIII. PROPERTIES

(a) Sparkling transparency
(b) Uniform quality and excellent machineability
(c) Amenability to printing/conversions
(d) Good barrier properties (vary with types) to moisture, gases, odour
(e) Moisture content – plain: 7–9 per cent,
coated: 7–8 per cent
(f) Oil/grease proofness: Good
(g) Shrinkage: 3-5 per cent
(h) Seal temp.: 100-130°C (Normal)
(i) Tear Strength: Low
(j) Flammability: Yes
(k) Flexibility: Good

Properties generally vary depending upon the type and grade of film. Different characteristics, however, can be built-up as per end-use.

THREE

LAMINATIONS IN FLEXIBLE PACKAGING

K.K. TALWAR

Laminations and laminates are of many different kinds in the world. In flexible packaging, however, lamination means the combining of two or more flexible web materials on roll to roll laminating machines in order to optimise physical and barrier properties of the combining materials. After processing the combined structure is slit or sheeted as the need be.

The main techniques of lamination process are extrusion lamination and adhesive lamination. Other methods include heat lamination, wax lamination, hot melting and co-extrusion.

Adhesive Lamination

This process consists of applying adhesive to one ply then combining with another before drying (wet bonding) or drying the adhesive and bonding the second ply with heat or pressure or both (dry bonding). Wet lamination is limited to those structures having one substrate that is porous such as paper. Adhesives like caseins, polyvinyl acetate or rubber latex are used for bonding (Fig. 3.1). Dry bonding is more versatile in that any two materials can be laminated once an adhesive system has been developed. The adhesives used now-a-days are a two component system like polyurathane or epoxy resin. This method involves low capital investment compared to extrusion lamination. However, the problems like solvent odour in case of dry bonding should be overcome and it takes about 24 hours for the laminate to be usable. Hence the quality of the bond is tested only after 24 hours. This is an ideal method for short runs (Fig. 3.2).

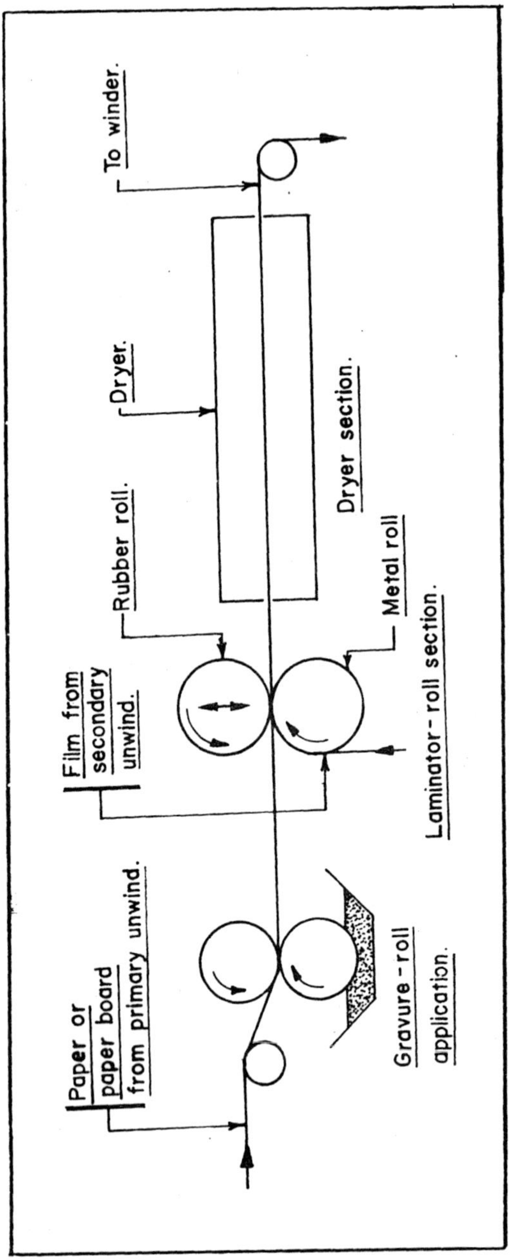

FIG. 3.1: Wet bonding of paper to film

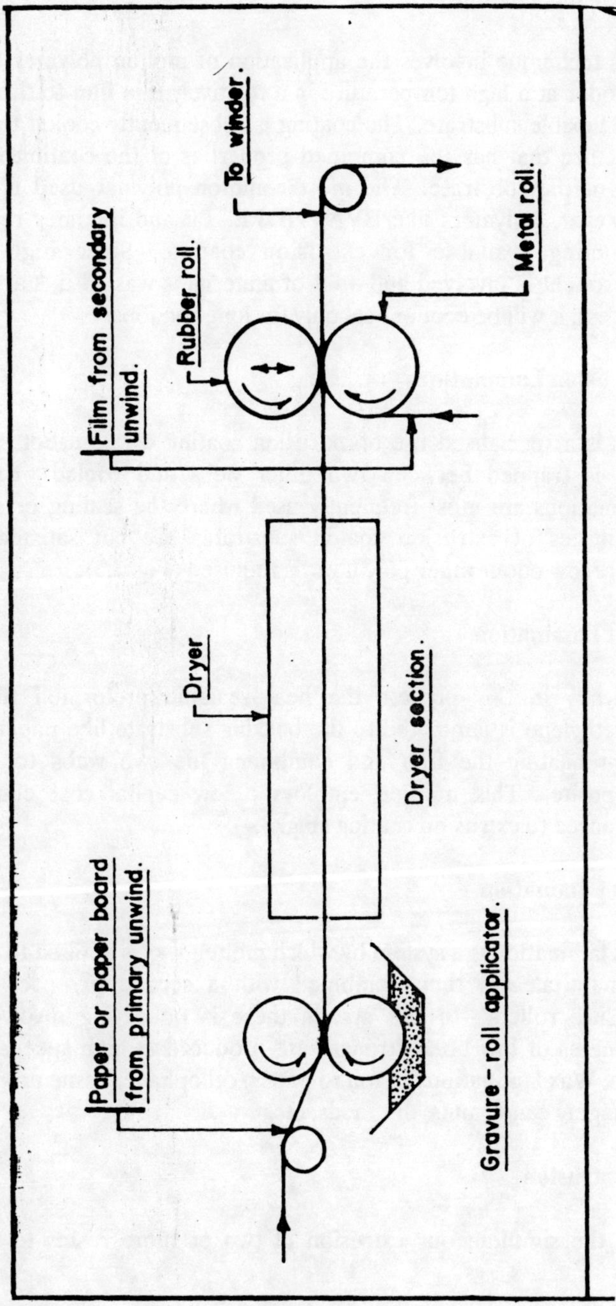

FIG. 3.2: Solvent dry bonding

Extrusion Coating

This technique involves the application of molten polymer from an extruder at a high temperature in a relatively thin film to the surface of a flexible substrate. The coating is subsequently cooled to form a structure that has the combined properties of the coating material and of the substrate. The most common polymer used is LDPE. However, polymers like EVA, HDPE, PP and ionomer resins are becoming available for extrusion coating. Since high capital investment is involved and a lot of material is wasted in starting this process, it will be economical only for long run jobs.

Extrusion Laminations

This is a specialised use of extrusion coating where a hot extruded film is trapped between two other webs and cooled. Extrusion laminations are most frequently used where the sealing or stiffness properties of extrusion coated substrates are not satisfactory or where low odour inner poly layer is required (Fig. 3.3).

Heat Lamination

Basically in this process the heat sealable preformed film like polyethylene is laminated to the backing substrate like paper or foil by preheating the film and combining the two webs to form a composite. This method employs a low capital cost equipment compared to extrusion coating (Fig. 3.4).

Wax Lamination

Wax lamination is a system by which molten wax is applied to one ply of material and then combined with a second ply over cooled pressure rollers. In this system there is no drying involved and laminates of low bond strength are produced at high speeds at low costs. Wax laminations of foil to paper/cellophane/tissue are used in packaging candy, nuts, dry foods, etc.

Co-extrusion

It is the simultaneous extrusion of two or more resins to form a

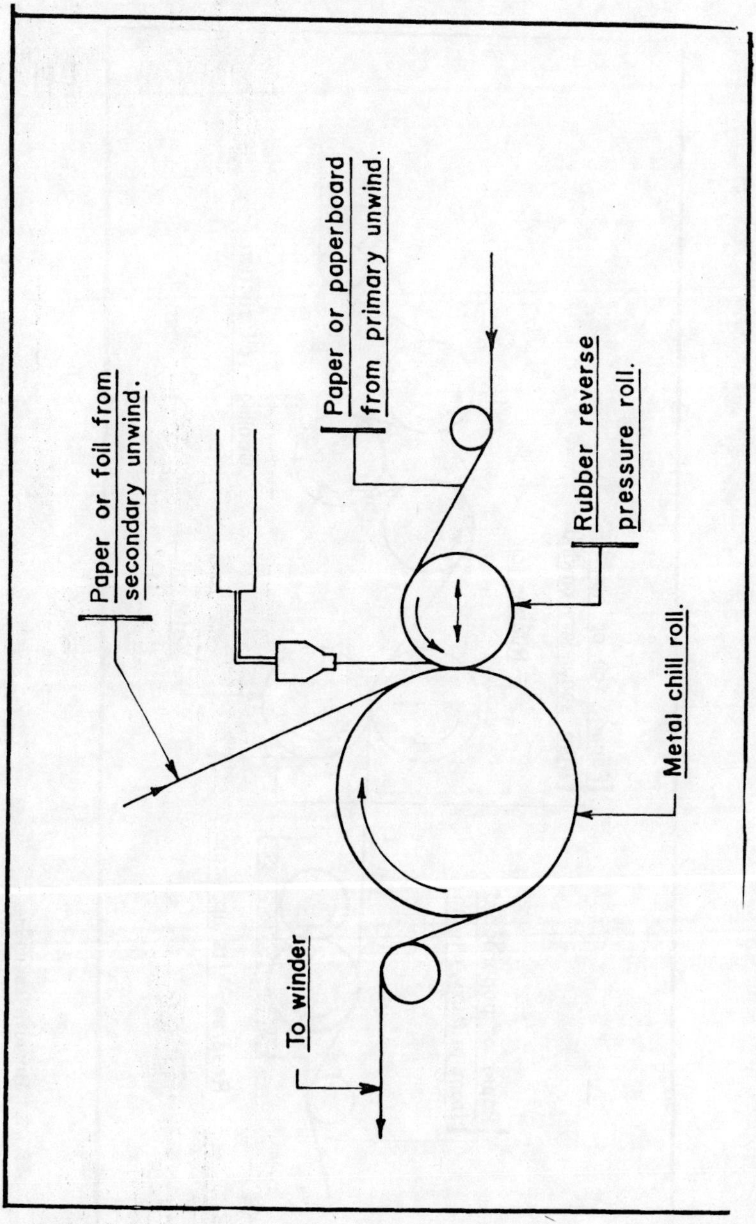

FIG. 3.3: Extrusion laminating

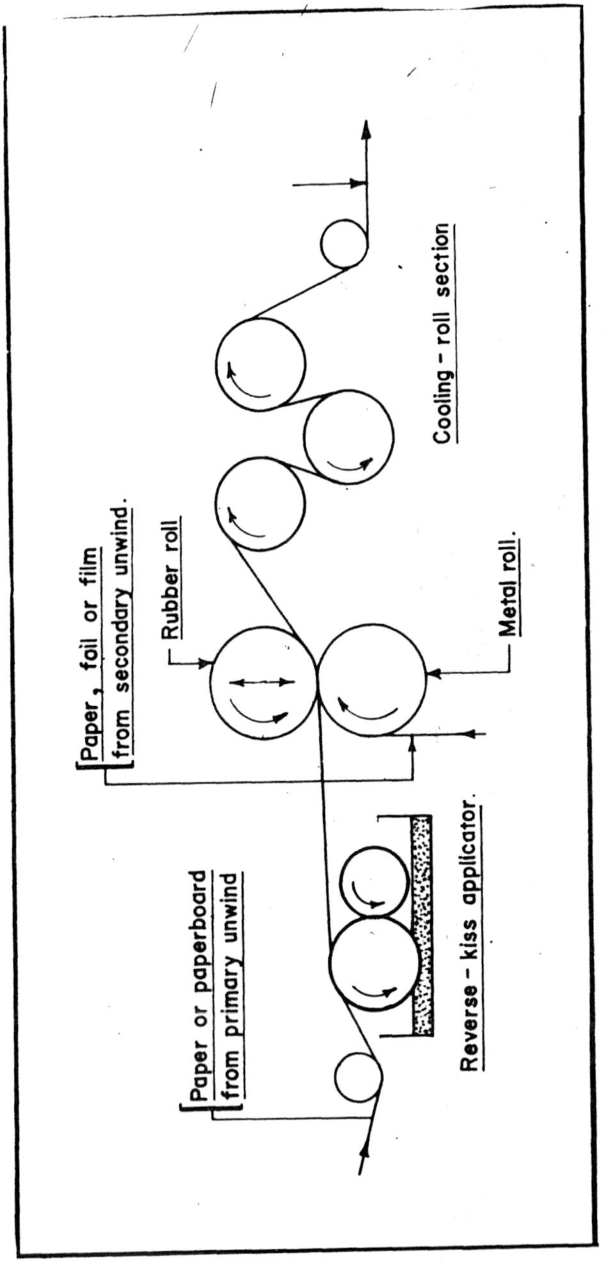

FIG. 3.4: Hot melt laminating

composite film. In this process two or more thermoplastic materials are extruded simultaneously through adjacent side die lips and combined either internally in the die or immediately after leaving the die. This single stage processing replaces other forms of lamination. However, the disadvantages of the process are the needs for large volume market, the high wastage levels incurred as well as technical difficulties in selecting the polymer that has specific adhesion and similar reheological characteristics. The process of co-extrusion is dealt in detail in the multilayer film chapter.

Why laminate? The answer to this question has many aspects. In Second, World War it was found that materials, specially food stuffs packed in the traditional packagings viz. glass bottles and tins could not be air dropped as they were heavy and brittle. When they were replaced by smaller packets of paper-foil-polyethylene, handling and air-dropping were easy. This packaging gave the same protection as glass or tin and further it was much lighter and did not easily break. After the war, this technique has never looked back.

Till that time the world was a much simpler place. The only plastic commercially available was polyethylene, which provided the sealant layer. Then there was development of new plastic materials which kept coming in the market. The emergence of different plastics has created a revolution in packaging, especially in flexible packaging. It was found that unlike glass and metal, which are absolute barriers, different plastics have different relative barrier properties under different conditions of temperature and relative humidity. There is no single plastic which can give the absolute protection like glass or metal. Each plastic has its own merits and demerits.

For example LDPE has a good moisture barrier property but no gas barrier property. It has good heat sealing range. HDPE has much better moisture barrier, little gas barrier, poor heat sealing range and more haze. PP and BOPP also have excellent moisture barrier, excellent clarity, but poor gas barrier and poor sealing properties. Polyester has a moderate moisture barrier and an excellent gas barrier and very good clarity and workability but it won't seal at normal sealing temperatures. Nylon has excellent oxygen barrier property and clarity but no moisture barrier. Laminates are more and more used in packaging application since by suitably combining different materials almost any desired combination of properties can be embodied into the construction properties such as moisture vapour resistance, gas barrier, odour barrier, light barrier, strength, scuff resistance, heat sealability, flexibility, chemical resistance, decoration, etc. Laminates invariably will achieve the balance of properties in terms of functional, physical and aesthetic consideration at a lower cost than it is possible in any other way. For example laminates of 25 micron cellophane and 25 micron polythene film produce a combination of properties which neither of these two films possesses individually in 50 micron thickness or in fact in any other film of that thickness. Thus relative properties of the different plastics available give us the tool to tailor make packaging to the shelf life required by way of lamination. This is what is known as optimisation production of the most economical structure for a particular requirement. This development has made a change in the whole concept of packaging.

A number of plastics behave differently under different conditions of temperature and humidity. The world has a number of different temperatures and humidity environments. This complicates problems for the modern packager. A simple BOPP bag will keep snacks crisp in Europe for two to three months but during monsoon in India such a packaging material will not make the product last for even two to three days. Simply following the recommendations of Western Countries can lead to commercial disasters. European agriculturists say, since their autumn harvest is followed by an icy winter, their seeds remain perfectly well for planting in the coming spring without using any costly packaging materials. Under our conditions of temperature and humidity, seeds deteriorate very quickly. Storage in gunny sacks may be perfectly safe in Europe but here it is most inadequate and can lead to wastages and poor germinating seeds.

Gas barrier plastics assume much greater importance in our country. Due to the higher heat and humidity not only things spoil quickly, but in a number of cases lose aroma or take up unwelcome aroma from outside to a much greater extent than in colder countries.

In order to get a really long shelf life of the order of glass or metal, one has to still incorporate aluminium foil in the structure. There is some talk in Japan about a flexible glass film being developed for the same purpose.

All of this means that technology has come into packaging to a much greater degree than before. You have to know your product much more and the properties of plastics and other materials in much greater depth along with the environmental conditions and marketing data. You have to then consider these different requirements and evolve an economic packaging for your product. Lastly since most plastics look alike, you have to have well equipped laboratories to test and find out whether the packaging material is as per the requirement.

Today the need is for technology of a high order to meet the rapidly changing scenario of the plastics world. A structure developed today may be obsolete in a year since a new and more economical combination may be available. This makes the world of flexible packagings more challenging.

FOUR

MULTILAYER FILM AND CO-EXTRUDED FILM, THEIR MANUFACTURE, PROPERTIES AND USE FOR FISH PRODUCTS PACKAGING

P.G.K. NAIR and R.S. RAMASUBRAMANIAN

Packaging – Introduction

1. Commercial applications of plastic films started about 85 years ago with the advent of cellulose based films. Plastic films have revolutionised packaging by offering well over 200 varieties of films with variation in moisture resistance, transparency, heat sealability and barrier properties in different environments. It is a paradox that polyethylene, a material mainly developed for radars during war period, now forms the largest outlet as a packaging material, due to its versatality, low price, transparency and strength. Plastics have taken big strides as packaging materials and their application in this particular form, as film, offers many of their advantages at a low cost.
2. The use of plastics in critical applications such as food packaging demands specific properties; which cannot be obtained from one polymer only. In recent years, the range of available polymers has been extended by special developments with regard to barrier properties, resistance to product action, sealability, strength, printability and adhesiveness. An impressive package is "half sold" but only a package which preserves the product for the intended application is "resold". Preservation methods are chosen depending on the product,

shelf life required and type of storage. Packaging of fish and fish products are extremely critical, since the products are highly perishable due to bacterial action. Here comes the role of the multilayer films. (Referred as MLF)

3. The advent of modern co-extrusion technology that can combine several layers of different materials in a single operation to give a "composite film" of outstanding performance, has given a big leap in their increasing use. In the following paper, the process of co-extrusion, properties of MLF, their applications for packing different range of fish products for domestic/export market and role of teaching/research/Government bodies in educating processors for proper packaging are covered.

Fish Products and Their Packaging Requirements

In the olden days, fish products were preserved by sun-drying and pickling. Now preservation of fish products are attained by controlling bacterial and chemical action mainly by freezing (conventional) or by freeze drying and keeping them in the good conditions by the use of modern methods of packaging. The packaging requirements for maintaining the sterile conditions and extending the storage life of the product are more critical and are achieved by the use of Multi Layer Films. Before explaining how the same can be achieved, it is advantageous to understand the manufacturing process and properties of MLF.

[1]

Co-Extruded Films and Multilayer Films

A film is a thin skin or membrane of a material of a planar form which is thick enough to be self supporting but of required thickness to be flexible, foldable and also convertible into various forms suitable for one or other of an enormous range of applications. Its metallic counter-parts are called foils and biologically derived forms are referred to as parchments or membranes. It is possible to obtain films of 1 μ metric thickness for special applications, whereas the upper limit of thickness can be anywhere from 100 to 250μ, depending upon the material. A few examples of films and their properties are illustrated in the Table 4.1, Part "A" of the table covers monolayer films, whereas part "B" covers co-extruded films.

---

1. μ = Micron (one millionth of a metre).

The monolayer films are made by:

1. Solvent casting
2. Extrusion and blowing
3. Extrusion and calendering etc.

Subsequent technology developments in extrusion field enabled simultaneous, i.e. co-extrusion of two or more materials to form a single composite film with the required diverse properties, which is called MLF. A drawing of the cross-section of a 5 layer film is given in Fig. 4.1.

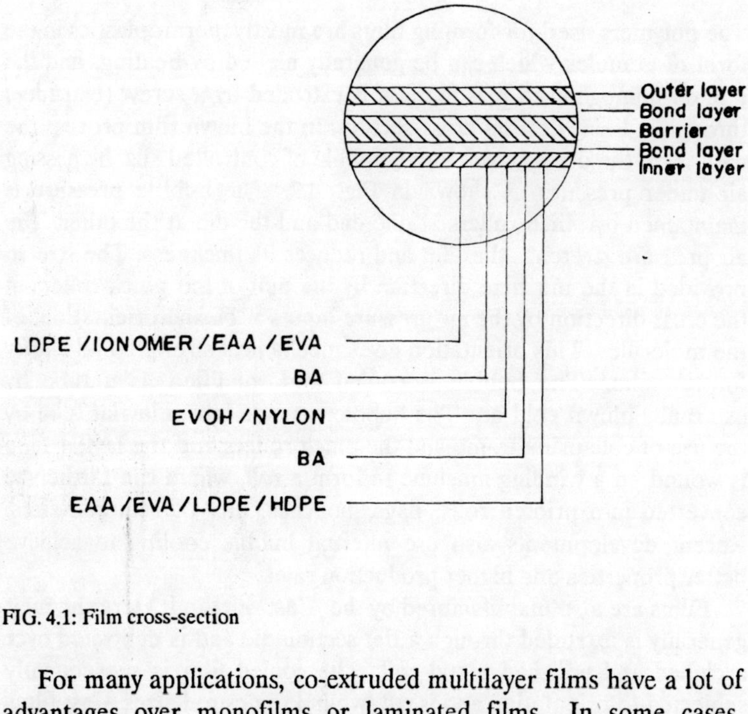

FIG. 4.1: Film cross-section

For many applications, co-extruded multilayer films have a lot of advantages over monofilms or laminated films. In some cases, co-extruded films are very competitive against monofilms due to improved strength at reduced thickness. In other cases, co-extruded film will win market shares from laminated films because it can be produced at lower cost in similar quantities and with better properties. Additionally, new application will be found for co-extruded films due to their specific characteristics.

Among the barrier properties, gas and moisture permeability form the basic requirements of a package. But none of the monolayer films are able to provide the required degree of gas/moisture barrier and sealing properties. Therefore, in the initial development effort, the process of lamination of two different films using suitable adhesives to obtain the required properties were attempted. For example, a film of polyester, which has excellent resistance to gas but does not have sealing property and LDPE which can resist moisture and has good sealing property were used to form a "laminate".

Manufacture

The polymers used for forming films are mostly thermoplastics in the form of granules which can be generally melted by heating, and the molten homogenised plastic mass is extruded by a screw (extruder) through a die of desired cross-section. In the blown film process the melt from the die is blown into a bubble of controlled size by passing air under pressure as shown in Fig. 4.2. The bubble pressure is maintained by pinch rollers at one end and the die at the other. The air pressure stretches the film and reduces its thickness. The stretch provided in the machine direction by the pull of the pinch rollers in the cross direction by the air pressure inputs a "biaxial orientation" of the molecules. This orientation gives mechanical strength and clarity for the film. The bubble is cooled and solidified as a tube by externally blown cold air. The bubble is made into a layflat tube by the use of collapsing frame and the pinch rollers and the layflat tube is wound on a winding machine to form a roll, which can further be converted into printed rolls, bags, pouches, etc. of required sizes. Recent developments also use internal bubble cooling to achieve better properties and higher production rates.

Films are also manufactured by the "Cast" method. Here the melt generally is extruded through a flat section die and is deposited over a chilled and polished metal roll. The cooled film is subsequently subjected to orientation and is cut/wound to desired sizes. Cast films have better gauge uniformity and optical properties. However, the equipment is costlier and has less flexibility, compared to blown film line.

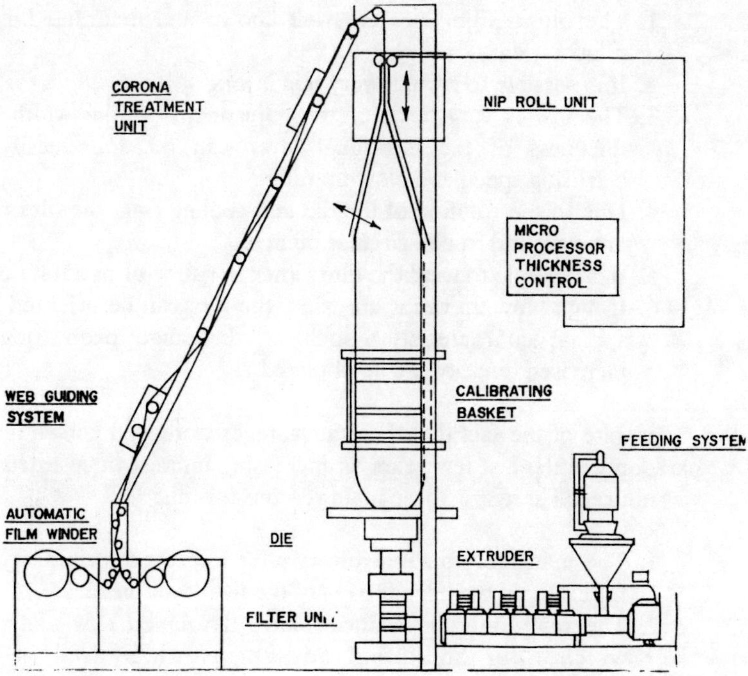

FIG. 4.2 : Blown-film line

Multilayer Films (MLF)

The conventional process of making multilayer film is by laminating or coating. In both cases, plain monofilm had to be bought or made and then converted. This procedure is discontinuous and has, therefore, disadvantages in regard to handling cost, storage cost, machinery cost and wastage.

In order to eliminate these disadvantages, the first coextrusion lines have been developed in the middle of sixties. These lines were able to produce multilayer films in one step, where two or more melt streams are joined when leaving the die.

For the coextrusion process, blown film lines as well as cast film lines are being used. The blown film process is mainly used for flexible packaging material with upto 200 micron thickness.

The advantages of the blown film process are:

1. The blown film lines are well known and their handling is relatively easy.
2. It is possible to extrude very thin layers.
3. The line is very flexible, the adjustment of film width and thickness of the individual layer can be done easily by extrusion speed and blow-up ratio.
4. Due to the rotation of the die and cooling ring, the film reels are even and free of circular bumps.
5. It is possible to wind the film either as a tube or as a flat film.
6. If high blow up ratios are used, the film can be oriented and special characteristics such as shrinkage properties or increased tenacity can be obtained.

In spite of the fact that these advantages were well known in the past, only in the last few years an increasing interest in co-extrusion was noticed. There are, three main reasons for this:

1. The machinery manufacturers offer improved technology, as for example the introduction of the five-layer die.
2. The raw material producers have developed new materials which offer additional advantages when used in the co-extrusion process.
3. The film producers want to improve their film quality and/or their economic situation.

The Fig. 4.3 shows a drawing of a co-extrusion line with four extruders used for a 4 component five layer film. The main difference as compared to single layer line described earlier is of course in the extrusion unit. Four extruders which are designed for extruding polyolefins and barrier materials are installed in a space saving arrangement.

The polyolefin extruders, normally for inner and bonding layer have grooved feeding parts. The barrier extruder for the centre layer and the extruder for the outer layer have smooth feeding inserts to extrude barrier materials of polyolefins depending on the requested combination. The melt streams coming from the extruders are led through filters into the rotation device and die.

The melt – leaving the die – is cooled by air. For this purpose the cooling ring is designed for uniform air distribution and high air velocity. For additional bubble stabilisation, air guiding rings are used which leads to the increase of bubble surface, just above the die. The follow-up equipment is similar to a standard blown film line with callibrating basket, collapsing frame and haul-off unit. All these parts can be controlled and set from the operating level by means of electrical motors and controllers.

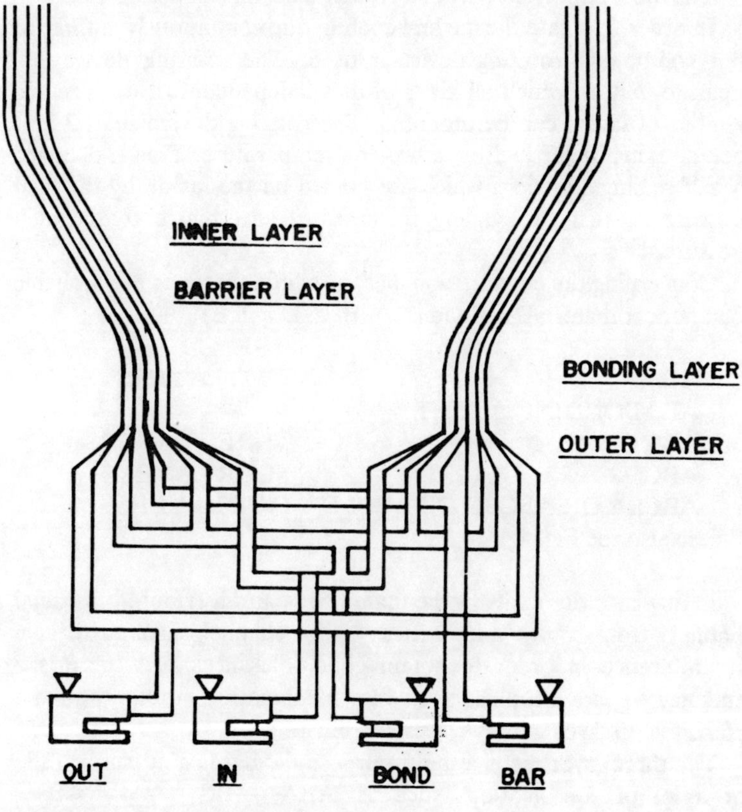

FIG. 4.3: Layer distribution inside die

The film is led from the haul-off station to the winder. Between these units additional installation like pre-treatment unit, guiding system and slit seal devices can be mounted. With such a blown film line, many different films, as for example thick and/or sticky films can be produced, it was necessary to optimise the winding station for these purposes.

Therefore, a new winder which can work as a contact winder as well as a centre driven winder is incorporated. The centre winder is especially required for sticky films in order to obtain smooth and uniform rolls.

This winder works automatically, the reel change is done after reaching the pre-set film length.

The most important part of a co-extrusion line is the die unit.

In order to rotate the die and cooling ring continuously, a three or four component rotating device is used. The rotating device is a separate unit on which all kinds of dies independent of die size and number of layers can be mounted. The rotating device seals 3 or 4 melt streams under high pressure and temperature. This is obtained by self sealing slip rings which are loaded on the inside by the melt pressure so that the sealing increases in accordance to the melt pressure.

Concerning the co-extrusion dies, five different types are available (component materials are named A, B, C, D and E)

AB	TWO LAYERS
AB + BONDING AGENT	
ABC OR ABA	THREE LAYERS
ABCD	FOUR LAYERS
ABCBA OR ABCBD OR ABCED	FIVE LAYERS

(Please also see Fig. 4.4)

In any case the melts of the main layers are distributed by radial channels from centre and then by spiral channels around the die circumference in order to obtain good tolerances. As there is a tendency to more sophisticated film combinations today the main interest lie in three and five layer combinations.

The three layer die is a multi-purpose die because it can be used for a lot of combinations such as: ABA, ABC, AAB, AB + BONDING AGENT.

The tolerances of each layer can be set separately. As a three layer barrier film has some disadvantage concerning handling, curling and barrier properties, the more progressive method for barrier film is a five layer construction consisting of 3 or 4 components.

The Fig. 4.4 shows the principle of a three component five layer film extrusion. The film construction is symmetrical, the melt streams of outer layers and bonding layers are divided into two streams by means of a valve block inside the die.

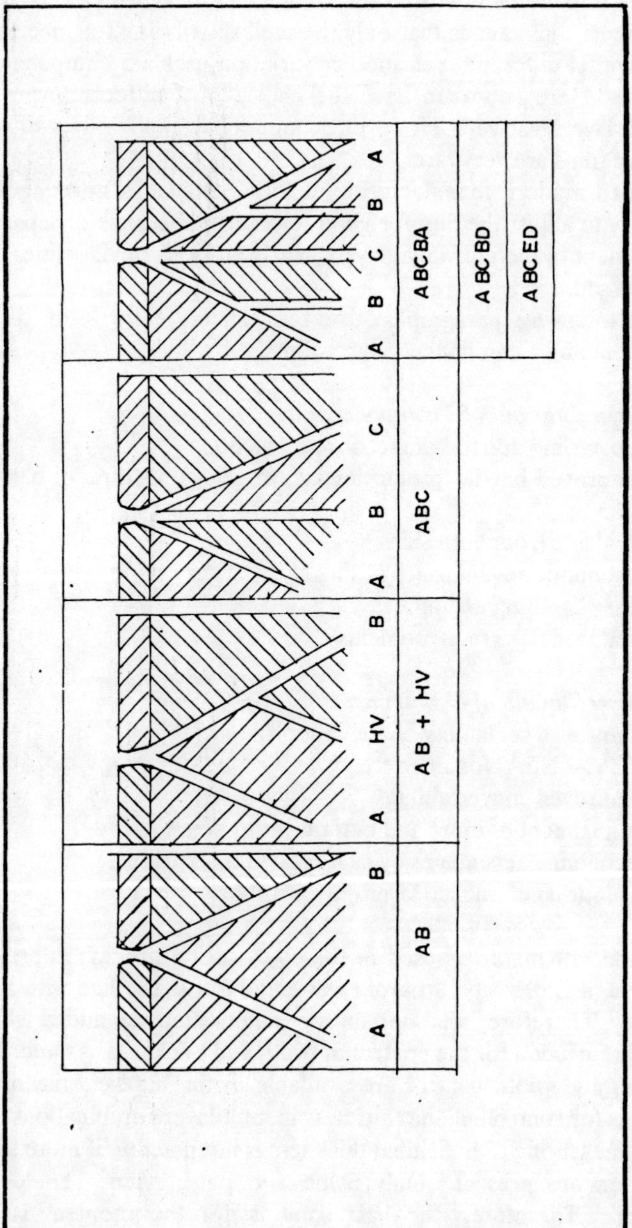

FIG. 4.4: Co-extrusion blown film dies

The same die can be used for 3 components as well as for four components, this means that only the melt distributor for inner and outer layer is different. Yet another variation uses a 5 component 5 layer die. Here, one can have the choice of 2 different types of bonding layers as well. However, commercial applications of this variety of films are very rare.

Due to modern manufacturing of these dies, it is normally not necessary to adjust the dies for good tolerances. Because of separate arrangement of the individual layers nearly all kinds of viscosities can be processed.

The following paragraphs give the salient features of the 3 component and 4 component 5 layer films.

5 layer films out of 3 components

- no curling due to symmetric construction
- improved barrier properties due to centre position of barrier film
- sealable from both sides
- economic advantages by using Nylon types
- easy handling and processing
- reduced flex crack problems

5 layer film out of 4 components

- improved sealability on the inner size (EVA, EEA, Ionomer etc.)
- improved convertability
- adjustment of inner and outer layer by screw speed
- economic advantages by LDPE layer on outside
- colouring of outside layer only possible.

As the raw materials used in the co-extrusion process often are expensive, it is desirable to avoid waste and to run the line with high efficiency. Therefore, some modules of automation are added which mainly are needed for the control of width and thickness. As units for thickness and width control are available in the market, the main interest is for controlling the thickness in multilayer combinations.

The measuring of individual thickness is not possible if more than two layers are present. Only nylon and polyethylene should be identified. Therefore, the best solution for the moment is an installation which measure the throughout of each extruder. In this case, a microprocessor is fed with production data such as line speed and film width so that with this information the actual weight of one metre of each layer can be calculated. In case there should be a difference between the gained values and the present weight, the screw of the individual extruders is adjusted accordingly. With this equipment, even very thin and expensive layers can be controlled and kept constant.

Raw Materials for Blown Film Co-extrusion

As mentioned earlier, the second factor for growing interest in co-extrusion is the development of improved new raw materials. Here should be mentioned:

- suporting materials
- bonding materials
- barrier materials

The supporting materials and their characteristics:

LDPE is still the most common material because it is transparent, easily processable, sealable, humidity resistant and has a relatively low price.

EVA is similar to LDPE but has better mechanical properties and better sealability. If the VA-content is more than 8 per cent the processability can be difficult due to sticky surfaces.

HDPE; High Molecular HDPE has good mechanical strength and better heat resistance. Due to reduced transparency, HDPE is mainly applied in the field of technical purposes as for example for heavy duty bags.

LLDPE has better mechanical properties and better sealability. The properties can additionally be improved by mixing with LDPE.

Ionomers/Acrylic Acid Co-Polymers

Due to their excellent sealing properties ionomers and acrylic acid co-polymers are used for special applications as for example, if films with thin surfaces having oily contamination have to be sealed. Also, types with special shrinkage properties are available.

Barrier Materials

Nylon is used as nylon copolymers or as Nylon 6. Nylon has good gas barrier properties, sufficient for a lot of packaging purposes in the food area and it has good mechanical strength. Today, nylon copolymers and also Nylon types with good transparancy are available, but due to the strong curling in 3 layers film, Nylon 6 can only be used in 5 layer films.

Polyester can also be used as barrier layer, but the low interest of the blown film market and the high processing temperatures are today the limitations for more efforts with polyester.

EVOH: This is one of the latest developments on the raw material market. EVOH has excellent gas barrier properties (about 30-50 times better than nylon). As this material is hygroscopic, the use as centre layer is recommended. The disadvantage is that EVOH is difficult to process and the lines require a special layout. As EVOH has insufficient mechanical properties this disadvantage must be compensated by combining it with materials with high mechanical values.

Properties and Applications of Multilayer Films

(A) *Properties*

The Tables 4.1 and 4.2 give the properties of various types of multilayer films.

Applications

The Table 4.3 shows some of the typical application areas for the 2, 3 and 5 layer films.

Fish Products Packaging

The conventional method used for packaging has been "Block freezing", overwrapping in polythene sheets and packing in duplex cartons. In this, products are almost invariably repacked at the receiving end into consumer pack sizes. A value added proposition would be to resort to the recent technologies like individually quick frozen pack with vacuum, gas flushing etc. Vacuum packaging enhances the shelf life of the frozen product by 6 to 18 months; depending upon frozen conditions.

TABLE 4.1: Permeability of mono-layer film and co-extruded film

Polymer/Structure	Thickness (Micron)	Density (gm/cm^3)	Permeability WVTR gm per m^2/24 hrs/ 37°C/90% RH	Permeability OTR ml (m^2.d.bar)
Part "A"				
CELLOPHANE	25	1.44	8	8
PETP	25	1.39	20	80
PA6	25	1.14	250	60
LDPE	25	0.92	20	6000
HDPE	25	0.96	5	2600
PP	25	0.905	8	3600
PVC HARD	25	1.35	20	120
PVDC	25	1.65	3	14
HIPS	25	1.07	60	6000
ABS	25	1.07	100	2000
IONOMER	25	0.94	30	6000
EAA	25	0.94	22	4500
EVOH	25	1.15	50	10
Part "B"				
LDPE/BONDING/ PA6/BONDING/LDPE	70	0.993	6	35
LDPE/BONDING/EVOH/ BONDING/LDPE	70	0.97	8	1

Gas flushing with appropriate gas or mixture of gases also helps to prolong shelf life and to retain colour of the flesh. In case of products that are brittle, gas flushing also helps cushioning the effects of transportation and prevent crushing and fragmentation.

Machine for vacuum packaging with or without gas flushing are presently available in India itself. Another range of marine products involves various drying processes. The recent trends are for use of freeze dried products. All dried products are advantageously packed in "High Barrier" films to prolong shelf life. Yet another range of marine products consist of prepared food items, based on marine products. Some of the typical examples are pickles, curries, extruded products etc. Some of these are packed in retortable pouches (Boil pouches).

TABLE 4.2: Mechanical properties of multilayer and mono-layer films

	Single layer thickness Mic	Total thickness Mic	Blowing proportion	Strength longitudinal N/mm^2	Strength transverse N/mm^2	Elongation longitudinal (%)	Elongation transverse (%)
Film Combination							
(LLDPE+LDPE)/ BONDING/ EVOH/BONDING/ LLDPE+LDPE)	52/5/ 16/5/ 52	130	1:1.4	26.7	21.8	260	290
LLDPE/BONDING/ EVOH/BONDING/ LLDPE	52/5/ 16/5/ 52	130	1:1.4	32.2	24.5	280	290
EVOH/HMHDPE/ EVA	15/100/ 15	130	1:1.4	26.9	22.8	500	730
LDPE/BONDING/ PA/BONDING/ LDPE	22/3/ 20/3/22	70	1:1.4	37.3	29.1	410	425
LLDPE/EVA	15/10	25	1:2.3	27.5	16	280	515
LLDPE+17% EVA		37	1:2.7	28.8	20.2	305	515
LLDPE+33%LDPE		108	1:1.5	27.1	14	520	520
LLD/BA/PA6/ BA/EAA	30/9.5/ 20/7.5/25	90	1:1.4	31.0	23	415	490
Monolayer Film							
LDPE		25	1:1.4	15	20	600	600
HMHDPE		25	1:4	45	35	650	450
HDPE		25	1:4	33	26	500	440
PAPER UNREFINED		25	–	7	25	5	5

TABLE 4.3: Typical application areas

Material combinations	Special properties	Most important fields of application
Two Layer Film		
1. LDPE/LDPE	Microscope-Tight-Multi Coloured	Milk Film, Carrier Bags, General Packaging
2. LDPE/EVA	Good Weldability, Sterilisable	Heavy Duty Bags, Stretch Packaging, Medical Articles
3. HDPE/EVA	Sterilisable	Blood Plasma, Bakery Goods, Foodstuffs
4. HDPE/LDPE	Good Tenacity	Bakery Goods, Foodstuffs Tomato Concentrate
5. LDPE/Ionomer or EAA	Good Weldability, Puncture Resistant	Dairy Products, Food Stuffs, Medical Instruments, Gen. Packaging
6. LLDPE/LDPE/ LLDPE/EVA	High Elasticity, Good Surface Adhesion	Stretch Film
7. Ionomer of EAA/EVA	Grease Proof	Coconuts, Biscuits
8. Ionomer or EAA/PA	Gas and Aroma Tight	Meat, Sausage, Ham Fish Foodstuffs, Cheese
Three Layer Films, Symmetrical		
9. LDPE/HDPE/ LDPE	Weldable on Both Sides Reduced Curling Tendency	Like 4, Pet Food Cornflakes
10. EVA/PP/EVA	Like 9	Like 9
11. EVA/HDPE/EVA	Like 3	Like 9, Cornflakes
Two Layer Film with Bonding Agent (HV)		
12. LDPE/HV/PA	Gas, Water and Aroma Tight	Foamed PS Granulate, Meat, Sausage, Cheese, Ham, Fish, Ready-made Meals, Hop
13. EVA/HV/PA	Like 12 IN Hot-Air Channel Hot Tack Welding	Like 12

(Contd.)

TABLE 4.3 *(Contd.)*

Material combinations	Special properties	Most important fields of application
14. MOD EVA/HV/PA		Like 12 Vacuum Packing for Ham (Shrinkable)
Three Layer Film		
15. LDPE/HDPE/ EVA	Good Weldability Good Rigidity	Bakery Goods Foodstuffs
16. LDPE/HDPE/ EVA	Like 15	Like 15
Five Layer Film		
17. LDPE/HV/PA/HV LDPE or LLDPE/ HV/PA/HV/ LLDPE	No Curling Tendency Improved Barrier Properties as PA Protected Against Moisture Absorption, Improved Layer Adhesion, Weldable on all Sides	Like 12
18. EVA/HV/PA/HV/ EVA	Like 17	Like 17
19. LDPE/HV/ EVOH/HV/LDPE	Like 17	Like 17 Fish Meal, Wine Packaging, Milk Powder (Casein)
20. EVA/HV/EVOH/ HV/EVA	Like 19	Like 19

* HV: Bonding Agent

Multilayer films can cater to all the above requirements in realm of flexible primary packaging. Several structures have been developed with contact layer materials like Surylyn, Primacor, etc. which have excellent resistance against almost all alkalies, acids, oil, fat, etc. They also have very high seal integrity resulting from their high seal strength and Hot-Tack strength. They also have the capability to "seal through contamination". For less critical applications, contact layer materials may be EVA, LLDPE, LDPE, etc. The gas barrier layer (oxygen, nitrogen, carbon dioxide etc.) is provided by materials such as nylon, EVOH, etc. and is primarily responsible for retention of vacuum or filled gases. The moisture barrier is provided by HDPE, PP, LLDPE, etc. and this prevents absorption of moisture or loss of moisture from the packed pouches. Depending upon the shelf life required and the type of products, various thickness of films are provided. The above films are also amenable for processing in almost all types of machines like Machine, Vacuum packaging machines etc.

Role of Education/Research/Government Bodies

When new generation packaging materials were not available in India, monolayer LDPE covers were used and the block frozen products were packed in duplex cartons and exported. By this process the products yielded very low value and thus the potential for large foreign exchange earnings were lost. And all the gains went to the repackers at the receiving end. Today, the latest generation packaging films like multilayer films and packaging machines are available in India. But even after these developments, major quantum of the export is being done as block frozen and by using LDPE films only. This calls for a sustained effort from the part of the Government bodies responsible for developments in the area to educate the industry on these aspects. By adopting the value added propositions by the use of the multilayer films our packaging will be of international standards and could thus target their efforts to the consumers pack markets like supermarkets, etc. and in the process earn more precious foreign exchange for same total quantum exported. With this in mind, we have elaborated the multilayer concept and its applications in fish products packaging. We are sure that all concerned persons in education, research, Government bodies would take appropriate measures to implement the modern packaging methods which will contribute to the need of the hour that is to improve the country's foreign exchange earnings.

FIVE

POLYMERIC PACKAGING MATERIALS AND THEIR SAFE USE IN FOOD CONTACT APPLICATIONS

R.A.N. MURTHY

In the field of food packaging, plastics have been a relatively recent entry compared to conventional materials like glass and metals. Plastics have not only revolutionised the science and art of packaging, especially in the field of food packaging, but have also been capturing those areas conventionally held by metals and glass. Further, plastics-based coatings are also used on glass and metal containers.

Some of the plastics commonly used for food packaging applications are polythene low density (LD), high density (HD), linear low density (LLD), high molecular weight high density (HMHD), polypropylene (cast and oriented polypropylene), polyester (PET), nylon and polyacrylonitrile (PAN).

All plastics, apart from the basic polymeric resin, usually contain several components (additives or adjuvants) either present as impurities or deliberately added for, in ppm to several per cent. These adjuvants can be of following types:

(1) Polymerisation residues (residual monomers and solvents, catalyst remnants, metallic impurities from manufacturing plants) which are unavoidable;
(2) Processing aids (heat stabilisers, antioxidants) to prevent thermal degradation etc., slip agents, lubricants, etc.;
(3) End-product additives which are deliberately added to the polymer either during manufacture or subsequently to achieve desired end properties in the finished product (e.g.

plasticisers, colourants, impact-modifiers, UV stabilisers).

Thus, the final processed plastics is a somewhat different material compared to the virgin polymer, and it is only natural to expect that it is the finished plastic material that needs to be evaluated by end-tests.

For example, the results of analysis of a molded polypropylene tub is shown below.

Non-polymeric components in a polypropylene molded article

Details	Concn. (ppm)	Origin
Polymerisation Residues		
Al, Ti, Cl	40, 5, 230	Remnants of Ziegler catalysts
Na, K	30, 18	Catalyst neutralisation. alkalies
Si, Fe, Mn, Ni	<20, 5, 0.1, 8	General contamination
Sn, V, Zn, Cr	0.3, 0.2, 10, 1	from the plant
C6-16 Hydrocarbons	900	Residual polymn. solvents
Propylene	1 ml/ml polymer	Unreacted monomer
Processing Aids		
Ca	40	Calcium stearate (stabilizer during molding)
Ionol	200	Thermal antioxidant
End Product Additives		
Barium	1000	$BaSO_4$ filler
Benzophenones		Light stabilizer
Dilauryldithio-propionate		Secondary antioxidant

The common leachable components from polythene, for example, are the antioxidants (e.g. BHT), lubricants (e.g. fatty acid amides), slip agents or colourants.

These non-polymeric components have the implications in the suitability of the plastic for applications involving contact with foodstuffs. Where direct contact occurs between the packed foodstuff and the plastic, it is likely that some transfer of adjuvants, which are of relatively low molecular weight, will occur from the plastic packaging material into the content thereby contaminating the product with the consequent risk of toxic hazard to the consumer. However, useful properties of plastics are not manifested without the additives. Therefore, to minimise the risk factor due to transfer of polymer additives, and also to restrict the ingress of non-nutritive substances into the food, the need for the formulation of guidelines for proper use of plastics for food packaging applications has been realised all over the world, and in view of the increasing use of plastics in food contact applications, such guidelines are also necessary to curb the indiscriminate use or abuse of plastics.

The primary concern of a regulatory body is public health. Therefore, the major requirement of the regulations is that materials for food contact shall be manufactured according to "Good Manufacturing Practice" so that under normal or foreseeable conditions of use they do not transfer their constituents to packed contents in quantities which could endanger the human health or bring about a deterioration in the characteristics of the food or unacceptable changes in its nature, substance or quality. Further, each type of flexible package has its own special technological problems and is best suited to specific foods. Therefore, for regulating their use, many countries have formulated standards and codes for the manufacture and use of plastics materials in contact with foodstuffs.

Basically, regulations on food packaging materials comprise:

1. Regulations for adjuvants (antioxidants, colourants, plasticisers, etc.) used in food packaging materials. Only cited materials must be used and within given limits i.e. the amount of the adjuvant which can be used and the kinds of plastic in which it can be used are prescribed.
2. Specifications for the basic polymeric resin used (residual monomer content, copolymer composition, some physical characteristics, etc.)
3. Extractive limits for the final food contact article (the limitations would thus include the contributions from all the adjuvants and processing aids used in making the food-contact packaging material, etc. These regulations spell out the

time/temperature/solvent conditions for the short-term extraction experiments ("migration tests") used to test compliance.

Therefore, a plastic material intended for food contact application must be of 'food grade' which means that only resins conforming to relevant specification and only permitted adjuvants must be used in the manufacture of packaging material. The regulations are regularly revised to incorporate necessary changes, if any.

Some IS specifications on plastics for food contact applications

Sl. no.	Plastic	Global Migration Limits*	Positive List
1.	Polyethylene	10146-1982	10141-1982
2.	Polypropylene	10910-1984	10909-1984
3.	Polystyrene	10142-1982	10149-1982
4.	PVC	10151-1982	10148-1982
5.	Polyester (PET/PBT)	12252-1987	12229-1987
6.	Nylon-6	12247-1988	12248-1988
7.	EVA	11704-1986	11705-1986
8.	Ionomer	11434-1985	11435-1985

* 10 mg/dm^2 and/or 60 mg/lit (ppm)

Miscellaneous Specifications

1. Colourants and Pigments 9833-1981**
2. Guide on suitability 10171-1986
3. Method of migration test 9845-1986

** As per IS:9833-1981, a plastic packaging material is not considered safe if colour migrates from the finished material.

The essence of this evaluation is a comparison between the Acceptable Daily Intake (ADI) of the additives which is derived from no effect level in animal feeding studies, and the maximum Estimated Daily Intake (EDI), i.e. the exposure which could result from the proposed use. The Food, Drug and Cosmetic act [Section 409 (c) (5)] requires that the "probable consumption of the additive" be considered in determining whether the proposed use is safe.

A knowledge of ADI is essential for fixing the limits for the amount of adjuvants that migrate from the packaging material. In order to determine the ADI, migration experiments are required which simulate, to the extent possible, the most severe proposed conditions of use and the maximum user-daily intake. In case of adjuvants, the results of these experiments are used to set limits on the concentration in the plastic so that exposure does not exceed acceptable limits.

For testing the EDI, ideally, migration tests for adjuvant transfer into foods should be conducted with each type of food in a given package under normal conditions of use for an expected contact of time. However, apart from being economically prohibitive, this type of evaluation with actual foods is analytically difficult because of their complex nature (food is generally a mixture of proteins, vitamins, carbohydrates, preservatives, etc. and these can interfere in the analytical methodology), foodstuffs vary in composition from place to place, and more importantly they are unstable and decompose fairly rapidly. Further, the duration involved makes long term tests with foodstuffs impractical.

Accordingly, special extracting liquids, called Food Simulating Liquids (FSL), have been recommended to be used in place of actual foodstuffs. For this, foods have come to be categorised into various groups, and the FSL chosen which may simulate the extractive character of the food class it is representing. Foods are mainly classified into four types: (1) Aqueous, (2) Acidic, (3) Alcoholic, and (4) Fatty. In Table 5.1 is shown the food categorisation and simulants.

TABLE 5.1: Food categorisation and food simulants

Standard food categorisation			Food simulant
FDA/USA	1)	Nonacid (pH > 5.0), acidic (pH ≤ 5.0), including oil-in-water emulsions of low/high fat content	Water (W)
	2)	Oils and fats; aq. nonacid or acid products with free oil or fat including water-in-oil emulsions	n-Heptane (H)
	3)	Alcoholic beverages (< 8% ethanol)	8% Ethanol (E)
	4)	Alcoholic beverages (≥ 8% ethanol)	50% Ethanol
BIS/India		Same as in FDA (USA) except for inclusion of 3% acetic acid (AA) for acidic foods	

Such extraction experiments are termed "migration tests". "Global migration" consider the total amount of the adjuvants migrating while "Specific migration" are concerned with specific adjuvants (Fig. 5.1).

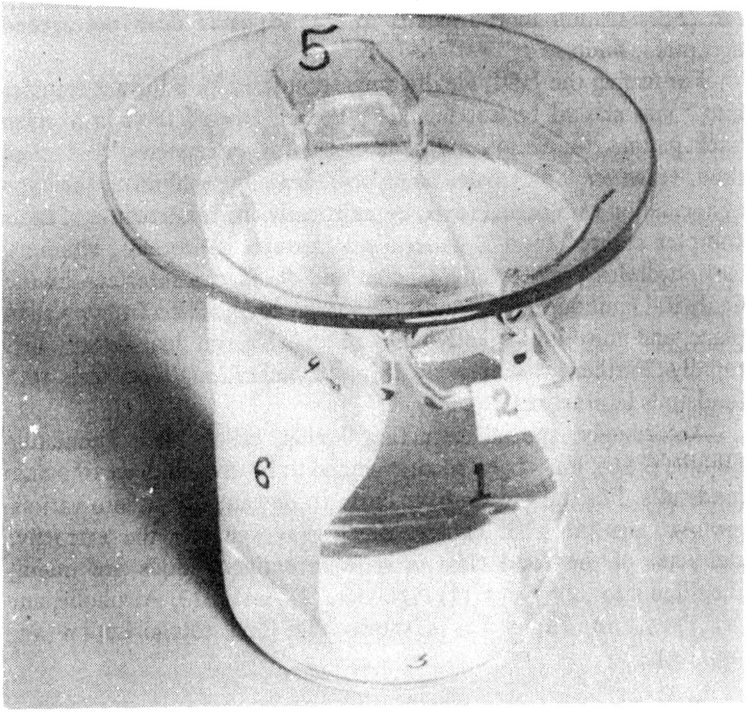

FIG 5.1: Extraction cell for determining global migration

The global migration tests are mandatorily prescribed in the specifications of all countries for food packaging materials. Global migration tests are important to test the compliance of a food packaging material to the extractive limits called "Global Migration Limits" (GML) in relevant specification. Table 5.2 lists the GMLs prescribed by various health authorities in world.

All plastic materials, intended for food contact applications, need to be first evaluated by migration tests before subjecting to shelf-life studies, etc. In migration experiments, time-temperature conditions are specified depending on the filling and storing conditions of the product. In Table 5.3 are shown the details of migration tests prescribed in specifications of various countries.

TABLE 5.2: Global Migration Limits (GML) in various specifications

Standard/Country	GML
BIS India BPF (UK), EEC	60 mg/kg or 60 ppm or 10 mg/dm^2 for all polymers for which specifications are available;
FDA USA	50 mg/lit or 0.08 mg/cm^2 for resinous and polymeric coatings;
	21-179 mg/sq. in for rubber articles;
	0.15 mg/sq.in (water) for phenol-formaldehyde molded articles;
	0.02-0.5 mg/sq.in for polyesters (depending on use-conditions) ;
	0.2-2.5 wt.% for various nylons depending on extractive solvent, etc.

TABLE 5.3: Time-temperature conditions in Global Migration Tests

Country	Test Conditions	Remarks
BIS/India[1]	1) 40 °C/24 h (W, AA, 8%, 50%E)	Long term contact
	2) 60 °C/2 h (-do-)	Short-term contact at high temperature
	3) 25 °C/30 min (H)	
EEC/ Europe[2] BPF/UK[2]	1) 70 °C/2 h (accelerated)	High temp. contact
	2) 40 °C/10 days	Long term room temperature.
FDA/USA[3]	1) 121 °C/2 h (W)	Sterilisation temperature
	2) 66 °C/2 h (H)	—do-
	3) 66 °C/2 h (W and 8% E)	Hot filled or pasteurised below 66 °C
	4) 49 °C/24 h (W and 8%E)	Room temperature filled and stored
	5) 38 °C/30 min (H)	Hot filled or pasteurised below 66 °C
	6) 21 °C/30 min (H)	Room temperature filled and stored
	7) 21 °C/48 h (W and 8% E)	Refrigerated storage
	8) 21 °C/24 h (W)	Frozen storage
	9) 100 °C/30 min (W)	Frozen storage: Ready-prepared foods intended to be reheated in container at time of use
	10) 49 °C/30 min (H)	—do-

1. Solvent volume 2 ml/sq.cm.;
2. Solvent volume 1 ml/sq. cm; and
3. Solvent volume 0.31 ml/sq.cm.

W: Water; AA: Acetic Acid; E: Ethyl Alcohol; H: Heptane

It is evident from the above Table 5.3 that conditions defined by BIS (India) do not clearly specify either filling conditions nor use conditions. With the advent of retort foods in Indian market, the test protocols need to be reconsidered and redefined because temperatures as high as 121°C are involved in actual processing.

As the migration of adjuvants increases exponentially with temperature, it is only to be expected that the test temperature is equal to, or better, more than the worst use condition. FDA conditions take cognisance of filling and storing conditions also. In this regard, there is a need to review the time-temperature conditions for migration tests presently in vogue in India and to prescribe test conditions closer to use conditions.

Methodology of Migration Tests

The procedure for migration tests essentially involves exposing the finished plastics food packaging material to the Food Simulating Liquid (FSL) under relevant test conditions. In case of films, a known area of the film is exposed to stipulated quantity of the FSL. In case of plain films, both sides of the film are exposed whereas in case of multilayer films, only the food contact surface is exposed (by making into the pouch form). For containers, they are filled to the brim, closed and kept under the test condition. At the end of the test period, the FSL is transferred to a container, concentrated to a small volume, dried in an oven at $100 \pm 5°C$ and the residue is weighed. The results are expressed in terms of mg/dm^2 and/or mg/lit (i.e. ppm).

One of the aspects which is assuming importance is the problem of residual monomers in plastics packaging materials. The problem is particularly severe in case of PVC because of the established carcinogenicity of the Vinyl Chloride Monomer (VCM). BIS prescribes a limit of 1 ppm in the resin and 10 ppb in food for VCM whereas the limits proposed by FDA (USA) is 5 ppb in the finished material. The determination of VCM at such low levels requires sophisticated instruments. Similarly there are limits for other monomers such as caprolactam in nylon, acrylonitrile in polyacrylonitrile, and VCM in PVC copolymers.

Thus, if export is intended, it is not just sufficient to test the materials as per BIS, but an examination of the specification of the target country is what is needed, and tests should be performed to suit those specifications.

Another problem which merits caution is the leaching of colour from coloured plastic packaging materials. In multilayer films, even though the colour layer is not the food contact layer but lies sandwiched, colour migration can still occur into FSL and even into oil. As per IS:9833-1981, a plastic packaging material is not considered safe if there is migration of colour from the finished material. It is apt to highlight here the necessity for layers other than contact layer also to be food grade including the adhesive layers.

The FDA permits the use of heavy-metal-content inks in flexible food packaging materials provided the inks are separated from the food by a barrier layer. However, the US Department of Agriculture (USDA) does not permit the use of such inks in flexible food packaging material even when they are separated from barrier materials because the usual barrier materials such as films, coatings, and aluminium foil are considered by the USDA to be inadequate to protect the food from these inks.

Still another factor which deserves care is the tainting of food contents by odorous adjuvants present in the packaging materials and subsequent effect on organoleptic quality. This is particularly true in case of PVC materials and polystyrene.

The Assessment of Safety

The regulations only apply to materials and articles which are in their finished state. No one may sell, import or use materials which do not conform to the requirements stipulated in that country.

The safety of an additive is appraised in terms of:

1. The extent of its proposed use
2. The amounts that would be consumed under all likely dietary patterns
3. The nature of biologic response it may provoke
4. The minimum intake that might provoke any response
5. Its nutritional contribution to food, and
6. The possibility of additive undergoing change after its contact with food because the altered additive may have a toxicity different from that of the original additive.

In view of this, Section 121.2500 of Subpart F of FDA states that

"An adjuvant can be contained in a food packaging material, but that such additive must be contained at the absolute minimum required to accomplish the intended physical or technical effect".

Once performance safety data have been evaluated for a specific packaging, the data do not need to be reevaluated when the packaging is sold to different processors provided the packaging and method of forming, including the processing conditions, are used without modification. As per the BIS, each batch of the specimen must be evaluated afresh for its compliance to GML.

There is no reason, however, for the packaging industry to feel unduly worried in light of the safety regulations. The food processing industry has a commendable safety record for shelf-life products in traditional glass and metal containers. However, a packaging revolution is now upon us that may and will alter the nature of packaging. If this occurs, the industry can still maintain the excellent record of safety by remembering that packaging, apart from being science, is also a "Responsibility".

For example, in the USA, the product safety record of flexible packages has been outstanding. With over 12×10^{10} packages (1986) produced there has not been a single incident of a fatality or illness attributed to container integrity.

SIX

FLEXIBLE PACKAGING MATERIALS FOR MARINE FOODS

K.R. KUMAR

Marine food products have special packaging requirements as distinct from fruits and vegetables, dairy products etc. The two broad groups to which they may be categorised are the fresh produce and processed forms. Further, the latter can belong to three broad groups:

(i) Dried products,
(ii) Intermediate moisture products, and
(iii) Product in liquid and semi-solid state.

Fresh Fish

Of all the flesh foods, fish is most susceptible to autolysis, oxidation, hydrolysis of fats and microbial spoilage. To preserve the quality, fresh fish must be refrigerated or frozen immediately after harvest. Any departure from immediate and continued refrigeration will lead to flavour and texture losses. (Malhotra, 1965).

Hence, a package intended for fresh fish must be able to retard fat oxidation and desiccation, protect against bacterial and chemical spoilage, eliminate drip and prevent odour permeation. For retail packaging, shallow trays with an overwrap of flexible packaging film is commonly used. If the product is large or irregular in shape, a direct film overwrap is used.

Tray packs are overwrapped with semi-moisture proof cellulose film (cellophane), polystyrene, oriented polypropylene or polyvinyl chloride. Molded paper-pulp tray is commonly used since it absorbs drip. Foamed (expanded) polystyrene, clear polystyrene or polyvinyl chloride trays require the use of an absorbent material. In order to obtain improved rigidity for direct film overwrapped packages, a plastic or wax-coated paper board insert is used. Improved shelf-life is obtained with a vacuum pack but this requires higher barrier films such as Saran (PVDC) coated cellophanes, polypropylene or polyester films.

Frozen fish requires a lower cold storage holding temperature than most other flesh foods like pork or beef. This is attributed to the fact that fish fats are more unsaturated and hence are more easily oxidized in cold store, producing rancid flavours more readily. The temperature used for cold storage has decreased over the years and varies with expected time of storage but -30°C is fairly standard for long term storage (Koizumi, C. et al 1978).

Package for raw frozen fish portions or fillets is mostly of polyethylenes, either as premade bags or wraps in Form-fill-seal machines, wax or hot-melt coated paper board carton with or without a waxed-paper overwrap.

Frozen fish may also be overwrapped in trays displayed in the frozen fish cabinet. Individual fillets are overwrapped with cellophane or PVC with and without paper-board inserts. In some cases, frozen fish is vacuum packed employing low oxygen permeable films to reduce rancidity.

A recent innovation in this aspect is the PVDC copolymer system for vacuum packaging whole frozen salmon. This system is claimed to provide a better alternative to glazing, which it cuts out altogether. It eliminates moisture loss on initial freezing and also during the first six months of storage, weight loss on glaze and reduces labour and time needed for traditional glazing plus drip loss on thawing. The lightly vacuumized package enables the salmon to retain its freshly-caught characteristics throughout the entire distribution system.

Controlled atmospheric packaging for fish is claimed (Bannar, 1978) to offer exceptional benefits with a vacuum/gas flush package for fresh fish. It has been estimated that the shelf-life of fresh fish might be extended to as long as 18 days.

However, it must be considered that vacuum packaging may give rise to anaerobic conditions which may be unsafe for fish products with a pH over 4.5 or less than 4.5 per cent salt content in the watery phase. Such products should be kept at a temperature below 4°C during retailing and preferably frozen.

Bulk shipment of iced fresh fish can be done in wooden boxes, corrugated fibre-board boxes and expanded polystyrene containers. As early as 1970, packaging and transportation studies on fresh fish were carried out by CFTRI. Improved insulated drip-proof baskets with coir insulation and polyethylene liners have been proved to provide adequate protective functions for economical transportation of iced fish. (Anandaswamy, et al 1971).

Corrugated fibre-board boxes used are generally wax coated. For further protection inner insulation may be used. Slab polystyrene foam is effective in providing increased insulation property, which is useful in keeping the product cold with a minimum of solid coolant (Govindan, 1981).

Processed Fish

Smoking or smoke-curing is carried out to add desired flavours, to inhibit microbial growth and to retard fat oxidation. Salting often accompanies smoking or it may be used as a separate method of preservation. Marinated fish are treated with vinegar and salt, usually with added spices.

A suitable package should prevent moisture interchanges and be impermeable to organic volatile flavouring constituents. The odour and flavour of cured fish may be lost through package permeability. In addition, there may be cross-tainting between different products in storage cabinets.

Sliced, smoked salmon is generally vacuum packed in transparent plastic pouches. It is also packed in laminated pouches of polyester/ aluminium foil/polypropylene. Most cured fish such as kippers, white fish and haddock are dried and more stable than fresh fish. They can be kept for several days unwrapped but hygiene and brand identification require on outer wrap. Recent developments in cured fish package include the use of nylon/polyethylene and polyester/ polyethylene laminated pouches. Boil-in-the bags for kippers in butter sauce or smoked salmon consist of polyester/ HDPE.

Another application of a plastic film in fish packaging is the 12 micron polyester film for items such as fish cakes in pillow pack style on FFS machines. This film is reverse printed and laminated to 50 micron polyethylene. This laminate possesses the barrier properties and puncture resistance over a wide range of temperatures.

Dry Fish Products

In salted and dried fish, deteriorative changes that occur are chemical changes such as protein denaturation, rancidity and browning, microbial changes and physical changes like the loss of texture. Most of these deteriorative changes are brought about by water-vapour absorption from the environment. Storage studies carried out on mackerel with an initial moisture content of 39.7 per cent, NaCl content of 14.55 per cent indicated shelf-life of 62 days when inside glassine + LDPE, PT cellophane + LDPE, MST cellophane + LDPE and 42 days in LDPE and stored at 38°C and 90 per cent RH. The shelf-life of the product stored at 25°C and 75 per cent RH was about 62 days in all types of packages (Sen, et al, 1960).

Fish protein concentrate (of whole red hake having 87 per cent protein, 0.1% fat, 10% ash) indicated equilibrium relative humidity (ERH) of 20 per cent at 6 per cent moisture content and 62 per cent ERH at 10 per cent moisture level, which can be considered as the critical level for good storage stability. (Rasekh, et al, 1971). Based on the water-vapour transmission rate values indicated, suitable packaging materials can be selected to provide the requisite shelf-life to the product (Fig. 6.1).

The packaging materials used for marine products are summarized below:

Product type	Packaging material	Packaging method
1. Salted and dried fish	HDPE, BOPP/PE	Air package
	PA/PE	Vacuum package
	PVDC/BOPP/PE	Vacuum package
	EVAL/PE	Gas packaging
2. Smoked fish	PA/PE	
	BOPP/PE	Vacuum packaging
	PET/FOIL/CPP	
3. Fish cake	Cello+BOPP/PE	Steam pasteurization
	PA/PE	
	PVDC/CPP/CPP	Vacuum
4. Fish sausage	PVDC Casing	Boil pasteurisation
	PA/PVDC/CPP	Retorting
	PET/CPP	Retorting

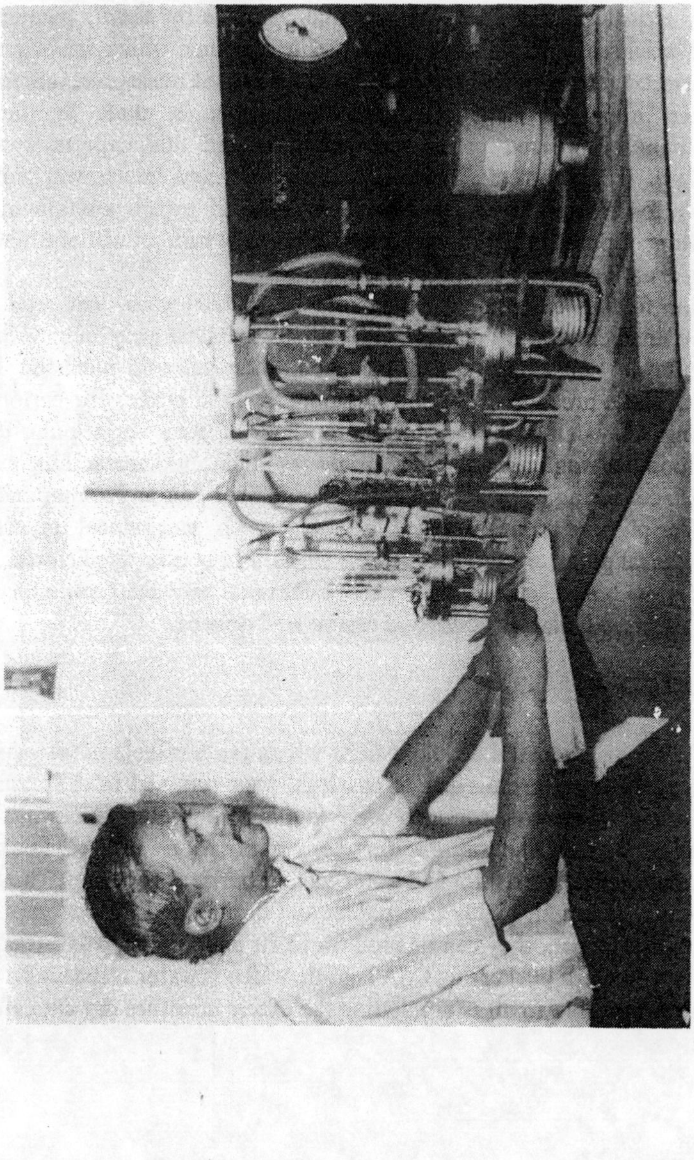

FIG. 6.1: Humidity chamber for the determination of shelf-life

Packaging Materials

Papers and Paper-boards

Paper and paper-board of specific grades are used in packaging of foods. Bleached kraft which has good strength properties is used as bags, sacks and liners. Grease-proof paper made by heavily beaten pulp has grease barrier properties while glassine which is super calendered grease-proof paper has good oil and fat resistance, odour barrier property. Vegetable parchment paper is made by the treatment of unsized paper with sulphuric and this imparts wet strength. It is non-toxic, fairly resistant to oils and hence wet and greasy foods can be wrapped in them. Waxed papers containing mixtures of paraffin and micro-crystalline waxes with or without hot melts are widely used in fish packaging.

For folding cartons, paper-boards of 200-600 g/m^2 are used. White lined chip board consists of bleached chemical pulp liner with other layers consisting of semi-bleached, chemical and mechanical pulps. These are one of the most commonly used grades for carton making. Clay coated boards have a top liner of pure virgin pulp. It has good bending characteristics, brightness and smoothness. Duplex boards consisting of bleached chemical pulp liner and underliner and middle plies of semi-bleached chemical with mechanical or all mechanical pulps are used for frozen foods. For special applications, solid white board having fully bleached chemical pulp liner and other webs is smooth on both sides and can be well printed.

Cellophanes

These are regenerated cellulose films which are available in various grades having different types of coatings, pigments and in different thicknesses. The most common MST film is a fair water-vapour and good gas barrier film suitable for many applications. MSAT films have better water resistant and water-vapour barrier properties. They are odour resistant, highly transparent and flexible and possess good sealability. Hence, they can be used for fillets and dry fish packaging. For very wet fish packaging, QSAT grade which is water resistant but highly permeable to moisture, letting the excess moisture dry out can be used.

Plastics

Polyolefins account for the biggest proportion of the plastics used in food packaging.

Low Density Polyethylene (LDPE) : It is the most commonly used material since it possesses many desirable qualities such as transparency, water-vapour impermeability, heat-sealability, chemical inertness and it is fairly economical. But organic vapours and oxygen and carbondioxide permeabilities are high and LDPE has poor grease barrier property. It resists temperature between -40°C to 85°C.

High Density Polyethylene (HDPE): It has a higher softening point than LDPE and is harder. Its barrier and mechanical properties are also superior to those of LDPE. High molecular weight high-density polyethylene (HM HDPE) has very good mechanical strength, less creep and better environmental stress crack resistance.

Linear low-density polyethylene (LLDPE) has better mechanical strength and heat sealability than LDPE. These properties can be made use of by blending with LDPE.

Polyethylene Modifications

Ionomers (Surlyn) which incorporate sodium or zinc ions as cross-linking agents are said to possess excellent sealing property even when contaminated with fats and oils, low-temperature resistance and hot-tack strength. Similarly, ethylene-acrylic acid copolymers (primacor) are claimed to give high strength seals and good adhesion to other substrates. Ethylene-vinyl acetate (EVA) which is similar to LDPE, has better mechanical properties, sealability and extension.

Another copolymer which has shown tremendous increased usage is ethylene-vinyl alcohol (EVOH or EVAL). It has extremely good oxygen and odour barrier properties especially at lower relative humidities as EVAL is hydrophilic in nature. When used as the core of a multi-layer material, it provides excellent performance in this respect. (Kumar, 1989).

Cast polypropylene (CPP) has excellent grease resistance and is also more resistant to solvents than LDPE. Polypropylene is not subject to stress cracking. Its softening point is higher than polyethylenes, and can withstand steam sterilisation temperature.

Polypropylene has low impact strength at very low temperatures but copolymer grades are available in which low temperature resistance is improved. Bi-axially oriented PP (BOPP) due to the orientation of polymer molecules in the two directions exhibits better tensile strength and barrier properties than CPP. However, effective tear resistance is decreased and heat-sealing property is affected. Hence, it is usually coated with suitable heat-seal lacquers or laminated to other webs to provide sealing property.

Vinyl Films

Among the vinyl films, Polyvinyl Chloride (PVC) is used in two forms, unplasticised as a rigid sheet material suitable for thermoforming and blow moulding, and flexible (platicised) in which form it is used for packing fresh produce. Rigid PVC is extensively used for making bottles, jars and thermoformed trays and cups as it has moderate gas permeabilities and good stiffness. However, its impact strength is rather poor.

Polyvinylidene Chloride – PVC copolymer (Saran) has very good water-vapour, gas and aroma barrier properties even as a coating, and hence it is used as an outer coating on other plastics such as PE.

Polystyrene is mainly used as a thermoformable sheet, generally modified by the incorporation of synthetic elastomers such as polyacrylonitrile and polybutadiene to improve the impact resistance. In barrier performance, it is quite permeable to water-vapour and moderately so to gases. Polystyrene cups, trays and portion packs are extensively used to pack sauces, pickles etc. foamed or expanded PS in thicknesses from about 200 to 2500 micron is used as a wrapping and for thermoforming into trays or fitments.

Condensates

Polyesters are a class of polymers, based on terephthalates. The most common and widely used one is polyethylene terephthalate (PET or PETP), although polybutylene terephthalate is used to some extent. PET has high mechanical strength and temperature stability and good gas impermeability. Generally as a film, it is used in thin gauges, about 12 micron to offset to some extent its high cost. It is used extensively as a metallised film. PET bottles and jars, especially stretch-blown grade have replaced the traditional glass containers in many food packaging applications.

Polyamides or nylons are a range of materials formed by the condensation of amines and acids. The most common polyamide is nylon-6 or polycaprolactam. All polyamides have good gas barrier performance, grease resistance and mechanical strength. But being more hydrophilic than polyester, they are more sensitive to moisture and quite permeable to water-vapour. Their major form of use is as co-extrusion webs with LDPE, ionomer and similar materials (Fig. 6.2).

The physico-chemical properties of plastic films and cellophanes are given in the Tables 6.1 and 6.2.

TABLE 6.1: Physical properties of packaging films

Packaging	Specific gravity	Tensile strength kg/cm^2	Elongation per cent	Tear strength g/25 mic	Bursting strength kg/cm^2 25 mic	Yield m^2/kg, 25 mic
LDPE	0.91-0.93	70.4-240	200-800	100-400	0.70	42.6
LLDPE	0.91-0.92	246-492	640-680	80-800	—	42.0
HDPE	0.95-0.96	173-357	10-500	15-300	1.40	41.2
HMHDPE	0.95	438-493	350-500	—	—	41.0
IONOMER	0.94	173-337	300-400	48-264	—	42.0
CPP	0.91	306-398	50-600	40-330	2.10	44.0
PVC	1.23-1.35	459-561	120-375	—	1.7-2.8	28.4-32.7
PVDC	1.65-1.69	844	40-100	10-20	1.4-2.8	22.7-32.7
PET	1.35-1.39	1785	70-100	13-80	3.2-3.5	28.4
NYLON-6	1.12	704-1264	250-500	20-50	7.0-12.6	34.1
PC	1.20	704-755	95-115	20-25	19.3	32.3
PS	1.05	357-847	1-3	5	3.50	37.1
EVOH	1.13-1.21	398-1601	235-325	400-500	16.2-23.2	32.6
EAA	0.94	430-454	520-545	374-467	—	41.8
MST CELLO	1.44	632-1264	15-23	2-10	2.1	29.4
MXXT CELLO	1.44	632-1264	25-50	7-15	2.0	29.4

1 M Pa = 10.2 kg/cm^2 = 145 psi
1 N = 0.1020 kgf

Metallised Plastics

Vacuum metallisation is the deposition of a thin layer of a metal such as aluminium on to other substrates. This process confers not only

FIG. 6.2: Determination of gas transmission rate

visual appeal, but significantly increases barrier properties to water-vapour (Kumar, 1983) and gases as well as the more obvious light-barrier and thermal reflection potential. Although any substrate could be metallised, PET and oriented nylons lend themselves best. The effect of metallisation on the barrier properties are given in the Table 6.3. (Dulin, 1978).

TABLE 6.2: Permeability characteristics of packaging films

Film	WVTR g/m^2, 24 hr. 38 °C/90% RH	Gas Transmission Rate ml. 25 mic/m^2, 24 hr. atm at 25 °C		
	25 micron	Oxygen	Carbon dioxide	Nitrogen
LDPE	18.6	7750	41850	2790
HDPE	4.6-10.0	2868	8990	651
IONOMER	19-27	4820-6850	9360-15500	—
CPP	7.8-10.0	2325-3720	7750-12400	620-744
PVC	3-40	124-465	310-465	16-155
PVDC	1.5-4.6	12-107	59-682	2-23
PET	20.1	47-62	233-387	11-16
NYLON-6	388	40	155-186	14
PC	150	4650	16682	775
PS	108-155	3875-5425	13950	1500
EVOH	22-59	0.5-20	0.7-24.6	0.02-40
EAA	22.3	4557	—	—
MST CELLO	7.8	8	6-93	8-25
MXXT CELLO	7.0	3	40-50	—

TABLE 6.3: Properties of oriented and metallised films

Film	Tensile strength kg/cm^2	Elongation %	WVTR, 1 mil g/m^2, 24 hr.	Oxygen-TR ml/mil m^2 24 hr.atm 25 °C
CPP	310-704	500-1000	10.9	3200
BOPP	527-2815	35-475	3.9	2448
Met. BOPP	-	-	0.4-0.5	14.8-34.4
NYLON-6	632-1265	250-350	248-340	39.6
BONYLON-6	2295-2500	100-120	155-171	18.6-21.7
Met BONYLON-6	-	-	6.4	3.2
BO PET	1408-2458	60-165	20	59.2
Met BO PET	-	-	0.3-0.5	6-16.8

Aluminium Foils

Foils of thickness 8 to 40 micron are generally used in food packaging. They are good barriers to gases, vapours and water-vapour even in lower gauges, which contain minute voids or pin-holes. They are absolute barriers in thickness of more than 25 mircons (0.025mm) and hence can be used for imperviousness. Foil as such is soft and susceptible for creasing. Hence, foil is generally used as an inner layer.

Composite Structures

Laminations

By the combination of papers, plastics, metallized films and foil, very large varieties of composite structures are possible, and different methods of production may be used. In any multilayer film, each component is selected for a functional purpose and often one material provides more than one property. Two or three component materials can be expected to meet most requirements, although larger numbers are used for specialised applications. Often, the printing is 'sandwiched' between two layers to enhance durability. (Kumar and Rao, 1980).

Co-extrusions

Various compatible plastics can be extruded simultaneously which fuse at the point of formation into a single web. It can be with either slot dies or annular dies. Where long runs of a standard material are required, and where reverse printing is not necessary, co-extrusion is the most cost-effective method. Generally, the 'barrier' film such as nylon or EVAL is made the inner layer to retain their barrier properties as they are susceptible for high relative humidities resulting in enhanced permeability rates and to reduce curling. (Soutar, 1987).

The effect of creasing and folding on the water-vapour and oxygen transmission rates for some of the commonly used films are given in the Table 6.4.

TABLE 6.4: Effect of folding and crumpling on the barrier properties

Water Vapour Transmission Rate				
	WVTR, g/m^2, 24 hr. 38 °C & 90% RH.			
	Flat	Folded	Crumpled	Gelboflex
Met PET (12 micron)	0.9	1.7	3.4	18
Met. PET/LDPE (50 mic.)	0.5	0.6	0.7	0.6
2-sides PVDC coated PET	4.2	3.7	5.9	4.8
2-sides PVDC coated PET/LDPE	2.9	3.6	3.3	3.1

Oxygen Transmission Rate				
	Oxygen transmission rate, ml/m^2, 24 hr. Atm. at 25 °C			
	Flat	Folded	Crumpled	Gelboflex
Met. PET (12 micron)	< 1	5.5	16	59
Met. PET/LDPE	< 1	< 1	2	3.5
2-sides PVDC coated PET	6	6	8	7
2-sides PVDC coated	7	7	9	11

(Dulin, 1978)

Testing and Quality Control

The following quality control tests are performed on packaging materials and finished packages to assess their physico-chemical properties. These data are useful in selecting suitable and compatible packages for packing specific marine food products.

Packaging Materials

- Tensile strength and elongation
- Tearing resistance
- Heat seal strength
- Impact strength
- Flex durabilty
- Water-vapour transmission rate
- Gas transmission rate
- Volatile transmission rate
- Grease resistance
- Tainting and Migration

Packages

- Drop test
- Stack load test
- Vibration test
- Shelf-life studies

REFERENCES

Anandaswamy, B., Raju, P.V., and Iyengar, N.V.R. 1971: Insulated drip-proof bamboo baskets for transportation of fresh fish with ice. *Packaging India*, 3, (4) 11.16

Dulin, C. 1978: Metallized films for food packaging. *Packaging*, 49, (574) 43.

Govindan, T.K., 1981: Packaging in fisheries-some musings, *Perfect Pac*, Jun-Jul, 12.

Koizumi, C., Iyama, S., Wada, S., and Nonaka, J., 1978: Lipid deterioration of freeze dried fish meats at different equilibrium relative humidities, *Bulletin of Japanese Society of Scientific Fisheries*, 44, 246.

Kumar, K.R. and Rao, A.R.V. 1980: Laminates for food packaging applications. *Perfect Pac*, 21 (9), 6-12.

Kumar, K.R. 1983: Water Vapour Permeation through polyester films and laminates. *Food and Drug Packaging* (USA).

Kumar, K. R. 1989: Recent Developments in Plastics for Food Packaging Trends in Food Science and Technology. *AFST (I)*, Mysore, 702-707. Eds.: Rao, M.R.R., Chandrashekara, N. and Ranganath, K.A.

Malhotra, S.S. 1965: Recent advances in processing and packaging of sea foods. *J.Food Sci. and Technol.* 2; 34.

Rasekh, J.G., Stillings, B.R. and Dubrow, D.L. 1971: Moisture absorption of fish protein concentrate at various relative humidities and temperatures. *J.Food Sci.,* 36: 705

Sautar, A.M. 1987: Flexible barrier packaging. *The Packaging Salesman*, 4 (Sr.no. 14) 9-14.

Sen, D.P., Anandaswamy, B., Iyengar, N.V.R. and Lahiry, N.L. 1960: Studies on the storage characteristics and packaging of sun-dried salted mackerel. *Food Science,* 10 (5), 148-156.

SEVEN

OPEN TOP SANITARY CANS: VERSATILE CONTAINER FOR FISH AND FISH PRODUCTS

K.K. BALACHANDRAN

Open Top Sanitary (OTS) can is a very familiar package in the food industry. The can preserves the food for a very long period and can be stored and transported in most adverse conditions without affecting the product inside. The can, though originally intended for thermally processed foods, is now increasingly being used for other items not thermally processed also. The versatility of the can is such that over 2500 different commodities are now known to be sold in cans.

Nicolas Appert, the inventor of heat processing technique of food preservation, used glass as container for his "Appertised" products. However, over the years the importance of glass as a container for canned fish, or canned foods in general, is on the decrease. Glass has largely been replaced by metal containers like tinplate cans, aluminium cans, etc.

Tinplate cans

The metal cans in the beginning were hand-made. Iron bars were hammered out to sheets of required thickness. The sheets after removing the oxide films by chemical treatment and washing were tinned by passing through molten tin. The tinned plate was marked and cut and made into cans. These cans had all the seams jointed by solder. Food was filled through a hole in the top and was later soldered in place. This 'hole and cap' container was difficult to clean and also posed problems in packing large pieces of food through a relatively small hole. Attempts to overcome the difficulties with this type of cans and the demands of the industry for a can which will facilitate increased production gave rise to the 'open top sanitary' cans which have a cylindrical body with soldered lock seam and unsoldered double seam ends. No flux or solder can come into contact with the food stuff packed and the easiness to clean make the can sanitary.

An ideal container for canned fish should have the following characteristics:

1. Strong enough to protect the contents adequately during shipment.
2. Readily fabricated into desired size.
3. Light enough for economical handling.
4. Readiy opened.
5. Impervious to air and water.
6. Of pleasing and sanitary appearance.
7. Not harmful or imparting toxicity to the contents.
8. Capable of being heated for sterilisation.
9. Inexpensive, preferably cheap enough to discard after use.
10. Readily hermetically sealable at high speeds.

Tinplate cans are most popular in use. Tinplate readily satisfies all the requirements mentioned above. Actually the term tinplate is a misnomer. It is in fact a sheet of iron plate coated on either side with tin giving a final composition of 98 per cent steel and 2 per cent tin. The thickness of the steel plate varies from 0.19mm to 0.3mm depending on the size of the can.

Tinplate is now available in many specifications and the can maker has to make the correct choice depending upon the product to be processed and the can size needed. The base steel plate used for making cans is referred to as the CMQ or Can Making Quality steel. The base plate used for can making should have the following qualities.

1. It should be capable of being rolled into thin plates which are ductile and able to take a thin coating of tin.
2. Coating of tin should be uniform reducing the porosity to the minimum.

3. Steel should be sufficiently strong to allow the cans to stand rough handling.

Corrosion behaviour, strength, durability etc. of the tinplate depends on the chemical composition of the steel. According to the Indian Standards specifications the base steel plate for OTS cans shall have the following compositions.

Carbon	0.04 – 0.12 per cent
Manganese	0.25 – 0.60 per cent
Sulphur	0.05 per cent max.
Phosphorous	0.02 per cent "
Silicon	0.01 per cent "
Copper	0.08 per cent "

As regards the corrosive nature of cans copper and phosphorus play very significant roles. The more of these elements present, the greater is the corrosiveness of steel. However, higher content of phosphorus will impart greater stiffness to the plate which is desirable in certain applications like beer cans where high pressures are developed. Generally a low metalloid content steel with a phosphorus content of 0.02 per cent called Type MR Quality is used in the manufacture of fish cans.

Manufacture of base plate

Can making is a multi-disciplinary technology. It involves different disciplines like precision engineering, metallurgy, corrosion science, lacquer, rubber, food, printing and other technologies like drawing, welding, soldering, etc.

The base plate for can making is made by the hot or cold reduction methods. Presently the entire world production of base plate is by the cold reduction process called the cold reduced plate (CR plate). CR. plates have the following major advantages over the hot reduced plates.

1. Superior mechanical properties.
2. More uniform, particularly in the gauge thickness.
3. Economical as it enables manufacture of cans out of thinner plates without loss in strength.

4. Improved resistance to corrosion.
5. Takes on uniform thin coating of tin.

Thin tinplate may require a modification in design and construction of the can to confer the rigidity needed. An improvement over the cold-reduced plate which possesses high tensile strength is called the double cold rolled or double reduced, also called 2 CR plate. This is made by subjecting the base plate to a heavy reduction in thickness during the final stages of rolling. After tin coating the 2 CR plate has a tensile strength upto twice that of conventional plate. However, because of its high strength and direction of the grain conversion to can components is more difficult than with ordinary tinplate.

Tin coating

The next stage in the manufacture of a tinplate can is the application of a thin coating of tin on the base plate. Two methods of tin coating are popular, the hot dipping and the electrolytic process.

Hot dipped tinplate

In the hot dipping process each base plate sheet is conducted through a layer of zinc chloride flux into the molten tin kept in a directly heated and thermostatically controlled tinning unit. The tinned sheet coming out of the molten tin is passed through a layer of palm oil. As the sheets pass through the palm oil they are given a "squeezing" action by tinned steel roles which largely regulate the final thickness of tin coating.

Electrolytic process

The base plate is cleaned well and is given a light electrolytic pickling in dilute sulphuric acid or dilute hydrochloric acid. This is then passed through a series of electrolytic cells filled with either dilute acid or dilute alkali. Pure tin is used as the anode. Direct current of required voltage and amperage causes the tin from anode to dissolve slowly and deposits on the cathode which is the moving base plate. The tin coating is dull in finish. It is then subjected to a momentary fusion by electric, conduction, radiation or high frequency conduction heating. An intermediate tin-iron alloy is formed at the interface and the tin surface becomes bright. The tin surface is subject to oxidation and in order to prevent this the tinplate is subjected to a chemical passivating treatment by chilling quickly and treating with chromic acid or sodium dichromate solution. After rinsing the surface and drying it is given a very thin coating of oil.

Thus, the tinplate is a steel base with four identical layers viz., the tin-iron alloy, free tin, the passivating film and the oil film on either side. The functions of each component can be summarised as follows:

1. *Steel base*

This contributes the mechanical properties of the finished product, that is strength and formability. The surface finish of the base plate determines to some extent the brightness of the finished product.

2. *Tin-iron alloy and free tin*

The corrosion resistance property of electrolytic tinplate depends mainly on the porosity of the coating. The tin-iron alloy, Fe Sn2, formed at the interface of steel and the free tin layer act as a bond between the two.

3. *Passivating film*

The free tin layer is liable to be oxidised in atmospheric conditions forming a yellow stain. A thin layer of chromium oxide deposited on the free tin layer prevents this oxidation thus preserving the bright finish over prolonged storage.

4. *Oil film*

A thin film of oil, usually dioctyl sebacate or acetyl tributyl citrate, is applied on electrolytic tinplate prior to its being sheared and packed. This permits easy handling as also prevents abrasion during transit.

Requirements of Thickness of Tin Coating

The tin coating thicknesses in the earlier days were expressed as units in pounds per Basis Box. A Basis Box is equivalent to the area of 112 sheets of size 20"X14" or 31,360 sq. inches. According to this terminology, a coating of one pound per basis box (also known as E. 100 plate) or 3/4 pound per basis box (E.75 plate) has been found satisfactory for processed foods. The requirements of tin coating thickness is now-a-days expressed as Grams per Square Metre (GSM).

Differential Coating

The requirements of tin coating weight will vary depending on the characteristics of the product to be packed and whether the can is lacquered or printed. The requirements may be different for internal and external surfaces of the can. Generally the surface where the food material comes into contact is given a heavier coating than the other surface. When the coating thickness is different on the two sides, it is called differential coating. Indian Standards Specifications recommended a differential coating of D 11.2/5.6 for fish cans indicating a tin coating weight of 11.2 GSM on one side and 5.6 GSM on the other. When the coating thickness is same on either side it is called even coating; e.g. E. 5.6/5.6 indicates a coating weight of 5.6 GSM on either side of the sheet.

Lacquering

With the expansion of the food canning industry it became evident that certain foods could not be packed in plain cans satisfactorily because of a reaction between the food stuff and the metal. Corrosion reactions ultimately leading even to perforation of the cans were observed in certain cases depending upon the nature of the contents of the can. Attempts made to cover the inside of the container with film of an inert material thus preventing the contact of the food with the metal led to the introduction of lacquered cans.

Two types of lacquers are generally used in food cans, the Acid Resistant Lacquer (ARL) and Sulphur Resistant Lacquer (SRL). The former is used mostly for packing red fruits and the latter for products such as meat, milk, fish, etc. which are rich in sulphur compounds.

Acid Resistant Lacquered Cans

Light coloured fruits are generally packed in plain cans where the presence of metal tin provides a brightening effect on the colour of the product which is a desirable quality. However, in the case of red coloured fruits they have to be packed in AR lacquered cans because the red anthocyanin pigments in them react with tin causing the fruit to turn purple and the syrup becoming cloudy. By packing in AR lacquered cans the fruit pigments are prevented from coming into contact with the tin.

In fact plain cans are less liable to damage from fruit acids than are the lacquered cans. In the former the tin coating is dissolved in preference to the steel base, so that hydrogen formation is much less than in lacquered cans. In lacquered cans, even if there is very little exposed iron it will be immediately attacked by the fruit acids, as there is only very little exposed tin to inhibit the reaction and hydrogen formation is comparatively very rapid. Oleoresinous lacquers are most commonly employed in fruit cans.

Sulphur Resistance Lacquered Cans

Products containing sulphur-bearing proteins some times yield low molecular weight sulphur bearing compounds during processing. In contact with tin or iron these sulphur compounds produce a black stain on the metal which can be tin or iron sulphide. In cases of extreme build up the black material may even get mixed with the product. To prevent the formation of this discolouration fish cans are coated inside with a sulphur resistant lacquer. Many types of SR lacquers are available, however, the most common for fish cans are the oleoresinous C-enamels. C-enamels contain zinc oxide which react with sulphur compounds liberated during heat processing producing zinc sulphide which is white in colour. The colour of the product thus remains unaffected.

Types of Organic Coatings

Majority of lacquers in general use are either oil-based (oleoresinous) or synthetic. The oil-based lacquers contain natural fossil gums and drying oils and are thinned with white spirit. Synthetic lacquers used for food cans are generally phenolic, epoxy, vinyl or polyester lacquers. Two recent introductions are the polybutadienes and diphenolic acid.

The lacquer used in food cans should have the following essential qualities.

1. Should not impart flavour or odour to the product (This consideration includes the factor of solvent removal as well as cure or proper bake of the coating).
2. It should be able to withstand high temperatures as high as 121°C or higher for long periods, say 90 minutes and above.
3. Coating should not degrade the colour of the product.
4. It should not absorb any colour from the product.
5. It should be resilient and elastic enough to stand the rigours of can manufacturing process, embossing of code etc.

Oleoresinous Lacquers

These are combinations of an oil or an oil derivative and a resin. Drying oils such as tung, linseed or dehydrated castor oil is mostly used as the oil base. The resins used vary from the naturally occurring resins, polymerisation products of unsaturated hydrocarbon materials, phenolic resins or combination of any or all of these. A lacquer having composition of approximately 50 per cent drying oil and 50 per cent resin have the required drying speed, adhesion, flexibility, and product resistance. To speed up the cure, metallic driers are used in the formulation.

Oleoresinous lacquers have perhaps the widest application in canning industry. They yield the typical gold coloured coatings on cans. When used without added pigments they are called "R" (regular) or "F" (fruit) enamels. However, when used along with 10-20 per cent zinc oxide and 90-80 per cent oleoresin the coating is called "C" (corn) enamel. Zinc oxide is added to induce the sulphur resistant properties.

The major advantages of oleoresins are their low cost and general applicability for food containers. The major disadvantages are their limited flexibility and failure to withstand many products.

Phenolic Enamels

Phenolic enamels are made of synthetic resin and solvent without drying oil. The resin is the reaction product of a "phenol" and formaldehyde. It is a common practice to add 5 to 10 per cent of high molecular weight compatible resin to improve its qualities. Phenolic resins have excellent corrosion resistance or resistance to sulphur staining products and exhibit good resistance to scorching during soldering and hence is ideal coating for both interior and exterior of fish cans. The important disadvantage of phenolic coatings is their extreme brittleness and poor flavour and hence they are mainly used as bulk linings for industrial products such as paints.

Epoxy Lacquers

Epoxy lacquers are synthetic resins prepared from Epichlorohydrin and biz-phenol. They have fair resistance to sulphide staining. However, they are not quite compatible with acid products which tend to undercut and lift them from the plate. They have excellent properties regarding fabrication, adhesion and flavour.

Polyesters

Polyesters are obtained by esterification of compounds containing hydroxyl and carboxyl groups. Polycarboxylic acids and polyalcohols are the starting materials. By proper selection of raw materials and by varying the reaction conditions, a wide variety of polyesters can be produced. These are acid resistant and do not impart any flavour to the acid products also.

Vinyl Lacquers

Vinyl lacquers are made of a synthetic resin and solvent. The resins are made by co-polymerisation of vinyl chloride and vinyl acetate. The vinyls have excellent properties regarding adhesion and flavour, but cannot stand the high temperatures of processing. They get charred while soldering. Due to their excellent properties with regard to flavour they are ideal for products such as beer and soft drinks which are not processed at high temperatures.

There are a number of other coating materials made of hydrocarbon resins, alkyds etc. many of which do not find use as internal coatings for foods cans. They find extensive application as a surface coat and as an excellent base for lithography.

Lacquer is applied to the tinplates by the roller coating method. After coating with lacquer the plates are baked at high temperatures, usually above 80°C for a predetermined time. Cross-section of an electrolytic tin-plate is shown in Fig. 7.1.

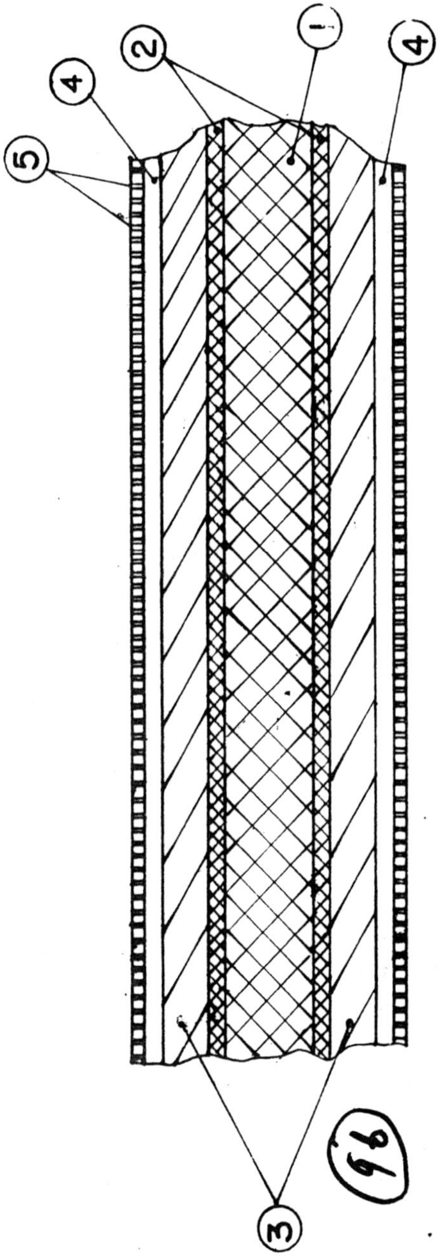

FIG. 7.1: Cross-section of an electrolytic tinplate

1. Steel base; 2. Tin-iron alloy; 3. Free tin layer; 4. Passivating film; 5. oil film

Fabrication of Can

Tinplate cans for processed foods in common use are the open top sanitary cans. They can be 'three piece' cans or 'two piece' cans depending upon how they are made.

'Three Piece' Cans

A three piece can consists of a cylindrical body with soldered side seam and two can ends attached to the cylinder by the method of double seaming. The operations involved in the fabrication are outlined below.

Body Making

Tinplate is cut to size for the type of can called the body blank. Care is taken to see that body blanks be cut absolutely square. The body blanks are passed through a flexing unit. This helps remove any irregularity in the sheet and also work hardens the sheet slightly. The corners of the blanks are then notched. By doing this, when the lock is formed, the ends of the seam will consist of only two thicknesses of metal, whereas the seam in between will consist of four thicknesses of metal. The blanks are then edged, by which a hook each is formed at the two shorter edges of the blank by bending one edge downwards and the other upwards. The hooks are then coated with flux and the blank is formed into a cylindrical body with the hooks locking tightly together. The locked hook is then hammered, applied with a second coat of flux to the outside of the lock seam and soldered in a solder mill. After leaving the solder mill excess solder is removed by a rotating brush. A splash eliminator ensures that the wipings do not contaminate the can following the one being wiped. A blast of cold air helps solidify the solder before the can body leaves the Body making machine.

The cylindrical can body is next flanged. The flanger consists of two flanging punches which fit into both ends of the can. These punches move slightly towards each other and force the edges of the body outwards thus forming flanges simultaneously at both ends of the can body. The sequences of operations involved in the process of can body making are schematically represented in Fig. 7.2.

FIG. 7.2: Sequences of operation in can body making
1. Notching; 2. Edging; 3. Forming; 4. Formed; 5. Flanged.

Can Ends

Can ends are stamped out from sheet tinplate and the edges are curled inward. To reduce the wastage of tinplate it is desirable to stamp out the ends in a staggered or scroll pattern than in straight parallel rows. The concentric expansion rings on the ends are simultaneously formed while stamping out the ends. The expansion rings will permit ready bulging of the ends during heat processing reducing the strain on the seams. The inside of the curl is lined with a sealing compound which is a rubber solution or emulsion or other material with good resilient properties. The ends are then passed through an oven for drying when a film of rubber composition is left in the groove and forms a gasket. This ensures an air tight seal of the finished seam by filling in the small irregularities between the metal faces in the can.

Lining Compound

Lining compounds are of two basic types, solvent base and water base. The solvent base materials are largely in use in food can ends because of the easy curing and the resistance of the compound to water.

Can Seaming

The can ends are attached to the body using a Double Seamer machine.

A double seam may be defined as that part of the can formed by joining the body and end components, the hooks of which interlock and form a strong mechanical structure. It consits of five thicknesses of metal, three thicknesses of the end component and two thicknesses of the body component. At the coincidence of the double seam with side seam there are seven thicknesses of metal and this causes a deformation of the end hook. However, this might have consisted of 11 thicknesses of metal had the body blanks been not notched, thus signifying the importance of notching.

A Double Seaming machine consists basically of three parts, a base plate, a chuck and a pair of seaming rolls, or grooved wheels which operate in succession. Of the seaming rolls, the one which comes in operation first has a deeper groove and the second shallower. The base plate raises the can body with the end in position causing the chuck to fit into the end of the can. The first seaming roll comes into operation and by pressing tightly and revolving at high speed round the curled rim of the end, tucks it under the flange of the body. The second roll then comes into operation and tightly presses and flatten together the hooked edge of the end and the body against the chuck, thus forming a final hermetic structure.

There are many types of double seaming machines whose designs vary according to the size and shape of the cans to be seamed. In many machines the chuck and base plate are caused to rotate whilst the rolls, being free to rotate on their own axes, approach the can radially to perform their functions. In other machines the chuck and base plate remain stationary, whilst the seaming rolls rotating on their own axes also rotate round the can and successively make a radial approach to perform their functions.

Basic design of a double seaming machine is shown in Fig. 7.3 and the profile of a can double seam is shown is in Fig. 7.4.

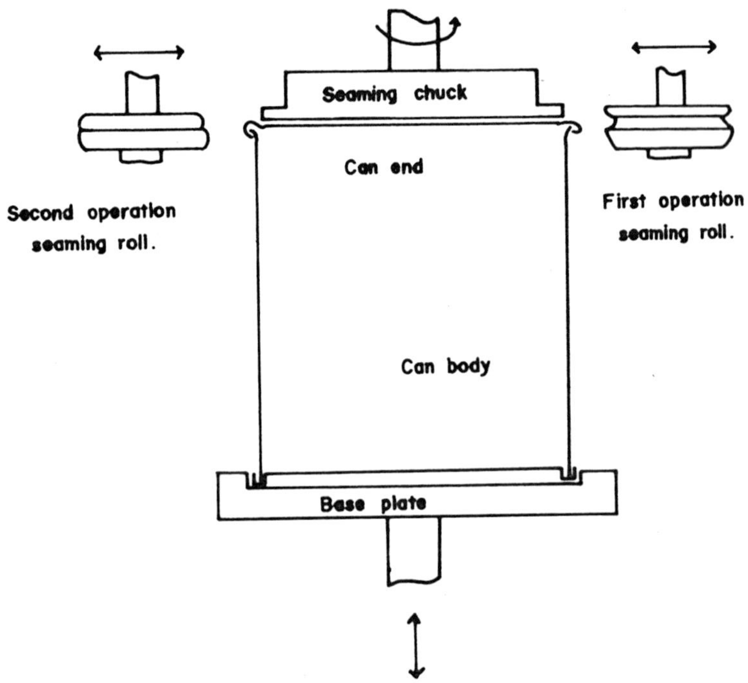

FIG. 7.3: Basic design of double seaming machine

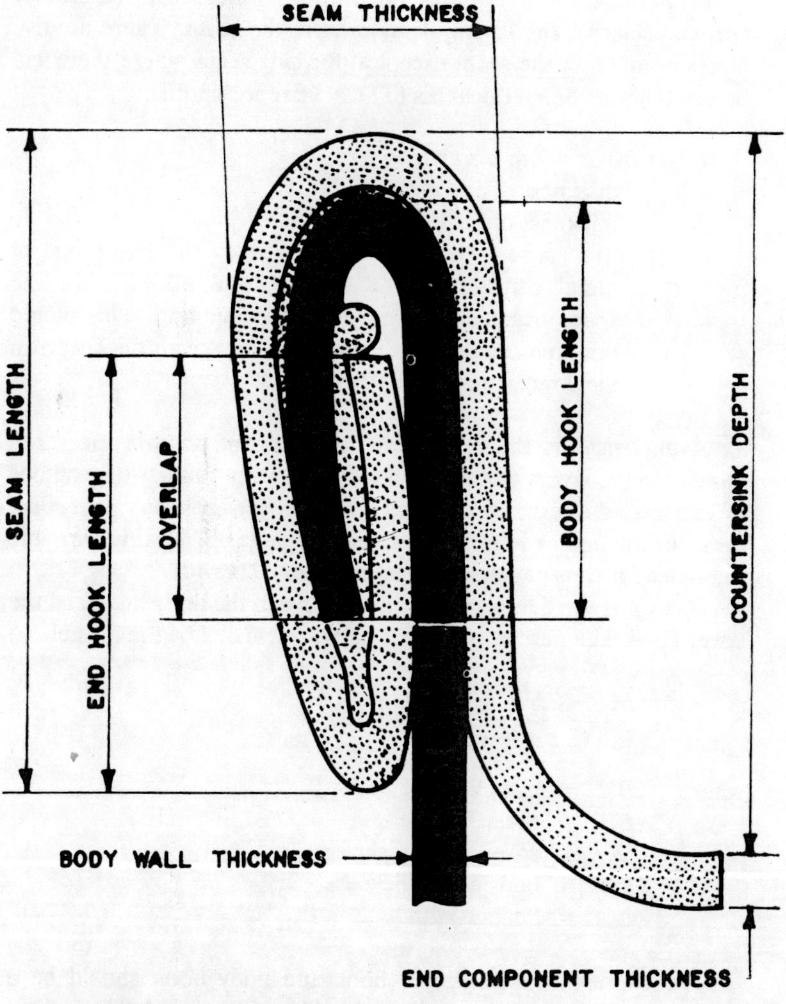

FIG. 7.4: Profile of a can double seam

There are very strict tolerances set down for can seams and the importance of a sound double seam needs no emphasis as no amount of good manufacturing practice and heat processing can compensate a faulty seam.

The important characteristics of a double seam are discussed below:

Seam thickness is the maximum dimension across or perpendicular to the layers of material in the seam. There are five layers of metal in the seam except at the side seam where there will be seven layers. Seam thickness (T) can be represented

T	:	$3\,tc + 2\,tb + G$ where
tc	:	thickness of end plate
tb	:	thickness of body plate
G	:	"free space", i.e. the space between the five layers of metal constituting the double seam allowing for the space occupied by the seaming compound. This should not be more than 6-10 per cent of the seam thickness; an ideal measurement is 0.0045".

Seam length is the maximum dimension of a seam measured parallel to the layers of metal and to some extent reflects the contour of the second operation roll. Seam lengths for cans vary depending upon the diameter of the can and is in the range 0.112" with allowable tolerance for cans of diameter varying from 202 to 401.

Overlap is the degree of interlock between the body hook and the cover hook. The percentage of overlap is calculated by the formula –

$$\frac{BH + CH + 1.1\,tc - L}{L - (2.2\,tc + 1.1\,tb)} \times 100$$

where

BH	=	body hook length
CH	=	cover hook length
tc	=	cover plate thickness
tb	=	body plate thickness
L	=	Seam length

The overlap between cover hook and body hook should be a minimum of 45 per cent; ideally it should be 60 per cent. The lengths of body hook and cover hook will be equal and ranges from 0.075" to 0.09" depending upon diameter of the can.

The countersink depth is the dimension of the seam that is measured from the top end of the double seam to the end panel adjacent to the inside wall of the double seam. It reflects the lip height of the seaming chuck, which acts as a suport for the can end and the body components during double seaming. The countersink depth should exceed the seam length by at least 0.005".

Droop: There is a slight increase in the seam length where it passes over the side seam with a corresponding decrease in the length of the cover hook caused by the extra thickness of metal in the side seam lap joint. The increased length of the seam at this point is called 'droop'. This should not be more than 20 per cent of the seam length in other areas.

The seam dimensions of commercially used round open top sanitary cans in India are summarised below (Table 7.1).

TABLE 7.1: Standard seam dimensions of some round OTS food Cans used in India

Diameter	Plate wt.	Seam dimensions in thousandths of inch		
	(lb per basis box)	Seam length	Seam width	Hook length
211	85	55-57	117-125	75-85
301	90	56-58	117-125	75-85
307	95	58-60	117-125	75-85
401	100	60-62	117-125	75-85
502	108	63-65	117-125	75-85
603	112	65-67	122-150	80-90

Some Common Defects Met with in Double Seams

1. *Cutovers:* Occur as a sharp fin at the top of the seam pointing inwards. This may occur at some points or all along the seam. This can be felt by running a finger round inside the seam. Cutovers could be caused by an excess of solder inside seam, a worn chuck, cocked can bodies, play in the seaming rolls and incorrect alignment of seaming rolls and chuck.
2. *False seams:* These are seams that are formed, but not hooked. They may appear normal form outside. This can be caused by knocked down flanges, damaged or bent covers or the container not centering on the seaming chuck.
3. *Incomplete seam* can be caused by the feed chain or the cover feed stroke operating out of time not synchronising with the movement of the can.
4. *Lips or excessive droop:* A droop on the seam at the side seam joint is normal, but a droop or lip forming at any other point

on the seam or excessive droop on the side seam is a matter of great concern. Droops can be caused by excessive body hook, the first operation roll being too loose, excess solder in the side seam or cocked bodies.

5. *Cut seam:* This is the phenomenon where the outer layer of the seam is fractured. The probable causes leading to formation of cut seam are too tight setting of seaming rolls, excess solder at the body lap, excess sealing compound and long body hook.
6. *Countersink too deep* is usually caused by exececssive base plate pressure, the chuck being set too low, use of improper chuck or covers, or the chuck fitting the cover too tightly.
7. *Countersink too shallow* is due to insufficient base plate pressure, the chuck flange being of a worn out nature, or the rolls and the chuck being out of alignment.
8. *Distorted countersink* (uneven countersink) can be due to cocked bodies, warped base plate, broken chuck or improperly formed covers.
9. *Finished seam too long:* This can be due to loose first operation roll or because the second operation roll is too tight or worn out.
10. *Finished seam too short:* This happens when the first operation roll is too tight or the second operation is too loose.
11. *Body hook too long:* This is caused when the base plate pressure is too high or due to improper seaming chuck height.
12. *Body hook too short:* Too low base plate pressure, too tight first operation roll, too loose second operation or improper seaming chuck can bring about this phenomenon.
13. *Cover hook too long:* The causes for formation of long cover hook are the first operation roll being too tight, shallow countersink or the base plate pressure being too low.
14. *Cover hook too short:* This can be caused by a short curl of the cover, a deep countersink, too great base plate pressure, or because the first operation roll could be worn, loose or tight.
15. *Uneven seams* can occur if the bottom seam is uneven, body is not evenly cut, the cover curl is not even or the can body is out of alignment at side seam.
16. *'Skidders'* are defects in seams caused by the incomplete second operation rollings.
17. *Wrinkling:* Wrinkles are formed during double seaming as the

diameter of the can is reduced. During the first operation puckers and pleats may be formed. During the second operation the wrinkles are distributed more or less uniformly around the circumference of the double seam. Normally an attempt is made to iron out the wrinkles. In round cans wrinkling increases with decrease in diameter. This is true of oval or curved rectangular cans where also wrinkles will increase as the radius of curvature decreases.

Excessive wrinkles indicate looseness of the seam. They extend from the edge of the base of cover hook. Therefore, extent of wrinkles can be taken as an indication of the tightness of the seam. The absence of wrinkles indicates 100 per cent tightness. A trace of wrinkle (80-100) is acceptable so that the seam is not too tight. The distance that the wrinkle extends on the cover hook is measured on a 0-100 scale. A rating less than 60 per cent is not regarded as commercially acceptable.

Two Piece Cans

Shallow profile cans made of aluminium and tin plate are popular for packing fish for many years. They are 'drawn' cans and are made by cutting, drawing and flanging in one operation. Tinplate used for drawn cans are heavier and more ductile than those used for round cans because of the strain it is subjected to during the drawing process. In two piece cans the bottom becomes an integral part of the can body and the lid is secured on the top by double seaming.

Two piece cans have the following advantages over the OTS cans.

(i) Elimination of two seams reduces the possibility of leakage;
(ii) Eliminates a potential source of lead contamination as no soldering is involved in its manufacture;
(iii) Has an aesthetic appeal presenting a smooth profile and streamline appearance;
(iv) The absence of the side seam permits uninterrupted external print decoration;
(v) Bottom of the can can be designed and formed to allow for better stackability; and
(vi) Elimination of the overlaps at the two seams results in use of less metal in its construction.

One disadvantage with the two-piece cans is the difficulty in the manufacture of tall cans. However, in recent years there has been considerable progress in producing drawn cans to effect overall improvement, particularly increasing can height. Drawn and Wall Ironed (DWI) can and Drawn and Redrawn (DRD) can are two classical examples of two-piece technology.

Drawn and Wall Ironed (DWI) Can

DWI can was developed in 1964 in the USA by the aluminium industry. Tinplate version became available by 1972. The manufacturing process involves the following steps.

(1) Blanking out a disc of metal from the sheet.
(2) Drawing the disc into a cup.
(3) Forcing it by means of a punch through a series of dies, each slightly smaller than the preceding one, thus elongating the wall by a stretching or ironing action. During this ironing process the wall thickness becomes reduced with corresponding increase in the height of the can.
(4) Trimming the top to the standard height.
(5) Washing to remove the lubricant.
(6) Flanging.
(7) Spraying internally with suitable lacquer.

Drawn and Redrawn (DRD) Can

The drawing operation for DRD can is traditionally performed by crank presses. In this process a blank disc is drawn into a cup, but the excess metal made available by reducing the circumferences of the body is used to elongate the wall, thus maintaining the thickness of the metal. A particular size can would be made by a series of press operations, the number being determined by the material used and the depth-diameter ratio. Thus, a shallow can could be made by a first draw followed by a redraw; a deeper can by a draw followed by two redraws.

In the DRD process the plate used must be pre-lacquered. The can wall remains substantially equal to the original plate thickness.

Aluminium Cans

By far, the most important and most extensively used alternate to tinplate container is the aluminium can used for packing meat and fish products as early as 1918. Aluminium used in can making is often reinforced by alloying with manganese, magnesium or chromium. Aluminium alloyed with manganese are mostly in use. Aluminium offers several advantages over the tinplate cans some of which are outlined below.

(1) Aluminium cans are light weight, little more than one third the weight of tinplate can of similar dimensions.
(2) Does not produce coloured corrosion products.
(3) Metal is non-toxic and does not impart metallic taste or smell to the product. It is not generally stained by sulphide bearing compoumds.
(4) Cans are easy to open.
(5) Good scrap value of the container after use.

Some of the disadvantages associated with aluminium cans are the following.

(1) Aluminium cans are not highly resistant to corrosion by acid fruits and vegetables.
(2) Aluminium is softer than tin-plate and must be handled with extreme care. It is also difficult to close body seams by soldering.
(3) Special precautions are needed during heat processing to avoid permanent distortion.
(4) Aluminium severely bleaches some products and service life is less than that of tinplate for most aqueous products.

Different methods are employed for the manufacture of aluminium cans like built up, shallow formed, deep drawn and impact extruded containers. Those used in fish canning are mostly made by the 'shallow forming' process. Aluminium cans mostly in use as containers for fish are the shallow round or rectangular cans. These cans are made in a single pressing process. Maximum height for a shallow drawn can is half its diameter and the maximum practical diameter is 150 mm.

Alloyed aluminium used in can making is first given an anticorrosive treatment, usually anodising in dilute sulphuric acid. The corrosion resistance of aluminium is attributed to the thin layer of oxide imparted by this treatment. To enhance the corrosion resistance this is further coated with a lacquer suitable for the products being packed.

Necked-in Can

A development worth noting in the two-piece technology of can making is the 'necked-in' cans. In this can the ends have the same diameter as the body. Such can do not over-ride one another and this give rise to high efficiencies on can lines.

Sizes of Cans

In commercial parlance the cans are generally denoted by a trade name followed by their dimensions denoted by a three digit symbol, the first of which represents the diameter of the can and the second the height. By accepted conventions the first number in the digital symbol represents integral inches and the next two digits indicate the measurement in sixteenth of an inch. Thus an A1 can which is, $2^{11}/16"$ in diameter and $3^{1}/16"$ in height is shown as 211X301. Now-a-days the dimensions are given in millimetres.

Trade names and dimensions of some of the popular open top cans in India are given in Table 7.2.

TABLE 7.2: Trade names and dimensions of cans used for fish canning in India

Trade name	Trade dimensions	Overseam dimensions
4-$^{1}/_{2}$ oz prawn	301 X 203	77 X 56 mm
8 oz prawn	301 X206	77 X 60 mm
1 lb jam	301 X 309	77 X 90 mm
No.1 Tall	301 X 409	77 X 116 mm
8 oz Tuna	307 X 113	87 X 43 mm
$^{1}/_{4}$ dingly	404 X 302 X 014 (L X W X H)	

Other Improvements in Can Manufacture

Several developments are taking place in the can making field either by way of introduction of newer materials for can or newer process in the can manufacture, all of which are aimed at increasing the efficiency of operations, reduction in cost and above all developing an appropriate container for a specified food item.

1. *Beaded Cans*

One way of reducing the cost of can is to use lower thickness plates. However, such cans may be deficient in the required strength. To overcome this, mechanical strength is introduced into the can body by beading. Fruit cans of capacity 5 to 10 kg have been introduced with this feature.

2. *Easy Open Ends (EOE)*

A very important development in the can making technology is the Easy Open End (EOE). First made for aluminium beverage cans, it was later introduced for aluminium cans for heat processed products like fish. Tinplate version of EOE also is now available. Tinplate or aluminium end prepunched with an aperture is sealed by an adhesive strip of metallised polyester film or aluminium foil.

3. *Cemented Side Seam*

Cemented side seam present a better appearance to the can compared to the conventional lock seam. This also permits for better seaming at the junction of the side seam. A thermoplastic cement (nylon bonding material) is used as the bonding material. This is applied to the pre-lacquered body blanks and a lap joint is formed which is bonded by the application of heat followed by rapid cooling. In order to avoid iron pick up by the food in the can the outside seam should be adequately covered by the nylon cement. The formed can is further sprayed internally with a coat of lacquer.

4. *Welded Side Seams*

This is a significant development in the can making technology on several counts. The 'Super Wima' welding technology is gradually replacing the soldering technology for OTS cans. Welded side seams significantly improve the can output. Besides, this yields a lead-free side seam. The narrow weld overlap consumes less energy and produces less heat which gives metallurgically better quality weld and improves flanging and double seaming operation especially at the junction of the side seam and the double seam. This technology requires less capital expenditure compared to other can making processes and there is also some saving in the can material because of the narrow overlap of side seam compared to interlocking hooks in soldered cans.

5. *Tin Free Steel (TFS)*

Tin free steel (TFS), also called tin free steel – chromium type (TFS-CT) is an important new introduction as an alternate to tinplate. TFS has a steel base with a chromium/chromium oxide coating on the surface replacing the tin in conventional cans. The appearance of the plate is bright or semi bright as compared to tinplate. Because of the low abrasion resistance of tin-free-steel it needs to be protected by a lacquer film. However, the surface of TFS provides an excellent substrate for lacquer adhesion which ensures superior performance in terms of product compatibility for many food products. The TFS cannot be soldered or easily welded without scraping chromium/chromium oxide coating.

6. *High Tin Fillet Can*

Certain vegetables, fruits and their products like spinach, asparagus, tomato products, dried prunes, green beans etc. have high levels of oxalates and nitrates and are therefore high detinners. These are normally canned in plain unlacquered cans. If canned in lacquered cans the colour of the products is affected. The HTF can was developed in the U.S.A. for canning such products.

HTF can is an internally lacquered can with a small tin fillet near the internal side seam. When the products are canned, small quantity of tin dissolved from the fillet protects the colour of the product and at the same time corrosion is prevented by internal lacquer.

7. *Light Tincoated Steel (LTS)*

A new type of tinplate called Low Tincoated Steel (LTS) has been made available with a very thin layer of free tin on the steel base, lower than the normal lowest coating of 5.6 GSM. The tin layer is further protected by a chromium/chromium oxide layer containing less of this than in the tin free steel. The tin coating weight is of the order of around 1 GSM.

8. *Grade 'K' Tinplate*

Aimed at improving the shelf-life of canned products a new type of tinplate developed and commercially used in the U.S.A. is called Grade 'K' tinplate. Grade K tinplate of 0.75 lb coating (16.8 GSM) usually gives a shelf life equivalent to ordinary 1 lb (22.4 GSM) plate for many products.

9. *Litewel-N (LTW-N)*

Another new can material is Litewel-N (LTW-N) intended for food and beverage products. LTW-N consists of a steel sheet thinly plated with tin and tin-nickel alloy. It is made into welded cans and is claimed to have corrosion resistance, weldability and lacquer adhesion comparable to tinplate despite containing less tin.

10 *Aluminised Steel Plate*

This is a can material prepared by coating aluminium by hot dipping or vapour coating process on steel plate. Soldered seam is difficult to get with aluminised steel and therefore welding or cementing the side seam becomes necessary.

EIGHT

RETORTABLE POUCH PROCESSING

K. GOPAKUMAR

A retortable pouch is defined as a flexible laminated pack having sufficient strength and heat resistance to allow it to be used in place of a can for the heat processing and storage of food products. Its essential properties are, therefore, well summarised in its alternate name: flexible can (Keith Jeffs, 1984).

History

The retortable pouch, as a substitute to metal cans, was first conceived, by the Continental Can Company in U.S.A., as early as 1948. However, the technology did not materialise, at that time, as suitable plastic materials were not available. The U.S. Army was always looking for a container of this type for their food supplies. The idea was revived in 1964 at the Natick Laboratories. Subsequently small group of companies representing the packaging industry (Continental Can), packaging machinery (Rexham) and food products (Swift and Pilsbury) worked with Natick Laboratories on a programme to develop a flexible can that could be used for army rations. Several companies in U.K., Europe and Japan made significant contribution in the development of retort pouch technology. The most notable among them were, Toyo Seikan Kaisha (Japan), Luigi (Italy), DRG, Metal Box and Bowaters (U.K.), Ruys (Holland) and Nielson (Denmark). But as expected retort pouch technology did not meet with success in the west. One major reason was the late approval of retort pouch by the Food and Drug Administration of U.S.A. The first generation pouches which were bounded by a conventional polyurethane adhesive (contained tolylidene di-iso cynate) doubted to be carcinogenic. Subsequently two alternate bounding systems were developed, one also essentially a polyurethane adhesive but contained alkyl isocyanate and the other a totally new process called "Morprime" which does not use any adhesive at all. Morprime process is based on the technique, dispersion of micronised polypropylene. Both these processes are safe and now cleared by U.S., F.D.A. for unrestricted use in food processing. But the delay in F.D.A. clearance occurred at the initial stages in the development of retort pouch became very critical and many companies which sunk millions of dollars in this field withdrew. By the time the U.S., F.D.A approval was given, industries were not prepared to invest again and the whole concept of a flexible can suffered a severe set back. Another reasons for the slow exploitation of the retort pouch is that, in Europe and the U.S.A., it had to compete with the well established canning and frozen food industries. Both in terms of cost and labour retort pouch processing is also expensive. However, in Japan, where canning and freezing industries were small, the growth of retort pouch industry was phenomenal. According to Japan Canner Association, in 1988, 1,27,704 tonnes of retort pouch processed food items were marketed. More than 50 per cent of them are curried foods and the rest sauces (Table 8.1).

TABLE 8.1: Retort pouched food packs sold in Japan in 1988

Unit Net weight : Tonne
Cases : 1000 case

Commodity	Net weight	Cases
Curry sauce	64,896	10,332
Stewed sauce	3,456	411
Hashed beef rice sauce	648	109
Meat sauce	5,704	897
Maabo tofu nomoto	5,619	930
Meat and vegetable dishes	3,033	874
Kamamesi nomoto	3,113	443
Meat products	4,440	492
Fishery products	3,846	451
Soup	5,078	708
Agricultural products	2,808	370
Rice products	2,238	414
Sauce products	15,428	2,821
Other products	6,415	744

Source: Japan Canner Association.

Advantages of Retortable Pouch Compared to Metal Cans

1. The retort pouch can be produced in any shape and size.
2. It has a high surface to volume ratio and a thin cross-section.
3. Rapid heat penetration is possible compared to conventional metal cans. Heating is uniform. In metal can overheating develops in the periphery and underheating in the core.
4. There is 30 to 40 per cent reduction in processing time.
5. Less impairment of texture and flavouring particularly of fish and meat products due to reduced exposure to heat. This results in better taste, colour and flavour of retort pouch product.
6. The retort pouch offers savings in terms of weight and space. Compared to an empty can, of the same volume, and empty retort pouch occupies 85 per cent smaller space and weighs 84 per cent less. Filled retort pouches also have significant space and weight savings compared to filled metal cans.
7. Retort pouches can be packed closely and tightly in master cartons. Hence, transportation is easy, safe and less costly. The shelf-life of retort pouch products is equal to or better than metal cans. Refrigeration or freezing is not required by packers, retailers or consumers.
8. Retort pouches can be easily opened by the consumers. There is no need for an expensive can opener.
9. Compared to metal cans retortable pouches are easily destroyed by incineration and thereby safe from environmental pollution. This quality makes it a versatile container for mountaineers, space travellers and also use for Arctic and Antarctic explorations.
10. The packets can be very easily reheated, prior to eating, by immersing in hot water.

Disadvantages

The retortable pouches have several disadvantages set against these merits.

1. The pouches are not robust like metal cans. Therefore, there is need for a strong protective outer pack. This makes total packing costs expensive.

2. Processing speed of a retort pouch line is slow. The outputs from current retort pouch lines are not as fast as that of canning lines. Some of the latest model of retort pouch lines have comparatively good speed of 200-240 bags/min. (Model – Toyo Jidoki Co. Ltd., Japan). However, this is no where near the speed of canning lines (400 packs/min. and above).
3. A retort pouch processing line is expensive compared to canning lines. The most expensive parts of the line are the form-fill sealing machine and retort. In the west, due to high cost of human labour, cost of retort pouch packs used currently is 40 to 70 per cent higher than cans while taking into account of both the cost of higher labour and outer pack. However, in countries like India, where there is no organised canning industry its costs are likely to be comparable if not less expensive. Countries like India imports either metal plate or cans. But the materials required for a retort pouch are produced indigenously. Consequently there is saving of valuable foreign exchange. The lower labour costs can also make the retort pouch processing less expensive.
4. Retortable pouches are susceptible to attack by rodents and insects, particularly in the tropics. They have to be safely stored. This is often a difficult proposition in India. Hence, it is difficult for retort pouch to make inroads in the rural markets.
5. Under processed packs can create enormous health hazards to people who are not aware of detecting spoiled pouches.

Despite all these disadvantages of retort pouch, in India, it can be a successful venture. Pouch making has become a very successful industry in India and in recent years most Indian converters, making pouches using locally produced raw materials, have shown record growth. More and more food products are entering in the Indian market and a pouch packed commodity has become an acceptable item to Indian consumers. This is a healthy trend. Hence, in the near future, like in Japan, retort pouch processed food items are likely to capture the Indian markets atleast in urban areas and metropolitan cities like Bombay or Delhi.

Composition

Majority of the pouches now produced are composed of 3 layer films.

This has polyester film on the outside face, a core of aluminium foil and an inner layer of a polypropylene copolymer.

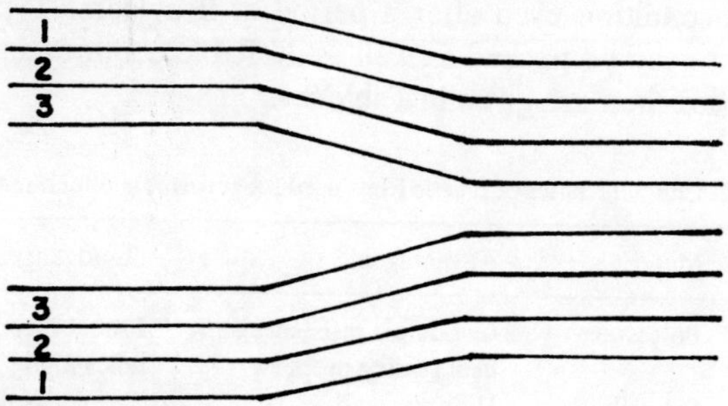

1. Polyester
2. Aluminium foil
3. Polypropylene

The core of aluminium foil is used to give the laminate the necessary water, gas, odour and other barrier properties. The foil thickness is normally 12 micron although 7, 9 and 15 micron foils are also used. The outer polyester film is normally 12 micron thick. Its purpose is to protect the foil and provide the laminate with strength and abrasion resistance.

The primary function of the polypropylene inner ply is to give good heat seals and product resistance. The polypropylene ply also protects the aluminium foil and contributes to the overall pack strength. The thickness of the polypropylene layer will depend, to some extent, on the nature of the product packed. While, for soft liquid containing products 50 micron films are used, packing products like sardines 70 micron film has to be used. Characteristics of films used to make retort pouches and composition of commercial pouches are given in Tables 8.2 and 8.3.

Stability of 3-ply Laminate

While 3-ply laminates are extensively used for packing various products, initial attempts in India have met with serious problems. Such pouches failed to give sufficient strength during processing and transport. It is likely that the type of items processed, particularly hot and spicy, may play an important role in selecting the number of plies needed. Our experience (Central Institute of Fisheries Technology) has shown that oil sardines packed in retort pouches having composition polyester/aluminium/ polypropylene remained in excellent condition even after a period of five years. Types of food items those can be packed as well as available commercially, packed in retort pouches, are given in Table 8.4.

TABLE 8.2: Characteristics of plastic films used for retortable pouch making

Layers	Materials	Advantages	Disadvanges
Outer layer	Polyester	Good heat resistance and heat sealing property	Probability of having pin holes high
	Biaxially oriented nylon	High strength	Shrinks during heat processing
	Non-oriented nylon	High strength and very good heat resistance	Difficulty in quality printing
	Biaxially oriented polypropylene	High strength and sealing	Develops shrinkage during heat processing; has the tendency to curl
Middle layer	Aluminium foil	High barrier	Pin holes, has opaque colour, poor heat sealing quality
	Polyester	High strength, heat resistant	Pin holes
	Nylon	High strength and impact resistance	Expensive
Inner layer	High density polythene	Good impact resistance High sealing property; cheap	Poor heat resistance, translucent
	Non-oriented polypropylene	Transparent, good heat resistance	Poor impact resistance
	Co-polymer of polypropylene and polyethylene	Good impact resistance, heat resistance, easy to seal	Expensive

TABLE 8.3: Types of commercially available retortable pouches and their composition

Type	Composition of layers	Type of lamination
I. *Aluminium pouches*	Polyester/Aluminium foil/ Polypropylene	Adhesive and "Moprime" lamination
	Polyester/Aluminium/ Special grade polyethylene	Adhesive and "Moprime" lamination
II. *Transparent pouches*		
a. Common	Polyester/Polypropylene Polyester/Polyethylene Nylon/Polypropylene Polyester/Nylon/Polypropylene	Both adhesive lamination and co-extrusion
b. Having high barrier properties (low oxygen permeability)	Nylon/PVDC; Eval/Polypropylene Polyester/PVDC Nylon/Polypropylene	
III. *Transparent trays*		
a. Common	Polypropylenes; HDPE/LDPE or LDPE/HDPE	
b. High barrier properties and (low oxygen permeability)	Polypropylene/PVDC/Polyethylene Polyester/PVDC/Polypropylene	
IV. *Aluminium trays*		
High barrier property (low oxygen permeability)	Polypropylene/Aluminium foil/Polyester Polyethylene/Aluminium foil/ Polypropylene	

PVDC — Polyvinylidene chloride

TABLE 8.4: Types of Indian products those can be packed in retortable pouches

1. Vegetable and fruits like pine apple.
2. Mutton curries.
3. Chicken curries.
4. Fish like sardines and mackerel in sauces and its own juice (natural packs)

**Commercially available products*

5. *Bhaji of PAV Bhaji* (Mixed vegetables in tomato sauce).
6. *Gajar Halwa* (Carrot pudding).
7. *Paneer Makhanwala* (Cottage cheese in tomato sauce).
8. *Alu Chole* (Chic peas and potato curried).
9. *Dal Makhani* (Lentils curried in sauce).
10. *Palak Paneer* (Cottage cheese in curried spinach).

* Trade names of some common Indian food delicacies, manufactured and marketed by M/s. Tasty Bites Eatables Limited, Bombay-400 018, India.

Retort Pouch Packaging System

The manufacture of retort pouch packs involves a series of lengthy operations. The essential process involves the following steps. The flow diagram is given below:

Flow Diagram of Retort Pouch Processing

Laminate rolls
↓
Formed Pouches
↓
Filling
↓
Shaping
↓
Tack seal
↓
Air removal
↓
Sealing
↓
Traying
↓
Retorting
↓
Detraying
↓
Rinsing
↓
Drying
↓
Outer packaging (Cartoning)
↓
Transit packing

Although each of the above operations can be done separately modern retort pouch processing factories employ integrated lines wherein all processes are done fully automatically. Details of the process is given below:

Pouch making

Pouches are conventionally manufactured by hot bar sealing and impulse sealing. Hot bar sealing is the way of directly sealing with a heated bar. Often a teflon coated bar is used to prevent over heating. Equipments which allows double, superimposed sealing followed by cold bar consolidation is preferable since this process ensures good seal integrity. There are excellent horizontal form fill and sealing machine available in the market. These machines automatically transfer these pouches to the filling rotary to open, fill and seal.

It is normal to round the corners of the retort pouches in order to reduce the risk of damage if pouches collide during handling and transport.

Filling

The process of filling can be done in two ways, either by hand or automatically using filling machines. While using large sized pouches for filling large sized food or solid, hand filling is often recommended. In automatic filling machines flat pouches are vertically held in position and a vacuum cup on each side of the pouch pull the valves apart their tops. Opening of the pouch is achieved by blowing air in the pouch. Exact quantity of the material is transferred to the pouch using an automatic weigher or counter. However, if the product to be filled is fish like sardines, which has to be arranged in the pack, there is little alternate to hand filling. During filling the following precautions have to be taken to avoid microbial contamination.

(a) The whole area should be clean.
(b) Keep the filling contents at the same temperature.
(c) The whole area and equipment should be free of micro-organism, particularly Salmonella, other pathogens and E. coli.
(d) During filling it is important that the closure seal area of the

pouch should not be contaminated with the products.

Deaeration

It is imperative that excess air inside the pouch should be removed prior to closure. The residual air in the pouch after processing should be less than 2 per cent of the volume of the pouch contents. Besides if too much air is left in the pouch there is a damage that it will inflate and burst during retorting. Excess air inside the pouch also impaires heat transfer and in cases results under sterilisation. Oxidative rancidity, particularly while canning fatty fishes, and consequent flavour changes are often seen due to excess air. Hence, it is imperative that excess air should be removed from the pouch.

Exhausting can be done by following methods:

1. Application of a vacuum sealing machine.
2. By injecting steam into the packs, to displace the air, and seal immediately.
3. To make it hot packed.
4. To spout out head space air by pushing both sides of the pouch a little to make the food level high. For filling liquid products this method can be successfully employed.

For filling solid products vacuum chamber sealers are suitable.

Sealing

There are two methods of sealing, hot bar sealing and impulse sealing. The hot bar sealing is accomplished by the use of hot metallic bar or bar coated with teflon. Impulse sealing is slow and not suitable for mass production. Pouches are now-a-days double sealed to reduce seal defects. Usually a first heat sealing is done under adjusted sealing temperature and pressure best suited to the material and thickness of a pouch. The second heat sealing is usually carried out under optimum temperature and pressure to complete the sealing to perfection. This operation virtually hermetically seals the pouch.

Seal cooling

During industrial retort pouch packing the heat sealed part of the pouch is mechanically cooled to make the sealing most perfect. This is done by pressing the sealed part of the pouch in a water cooled press.

Traying

The filled and sealed packs should be laid flat on the retort trays. These trays, should be pocketed to prevent movement and super imposition during retorting.

Retorting

Heat sterilisation of the filled and sealed pouch is done in retorts using steam-air mixture. Although the sealed pouch can withstand external pressure, a slight difference in internal pressure even to the order of 0.1 kg/cm^2, can result to bursting of the pouch. Pressure developed inside the retort is high. Actual process time for each product has to be determined by heat penetration tests (Table 8.5).

TABLE 8.5: Retorting temperature and time of some fish products

Product	Pouch size (mm)	Processing	
		Temp. °C	Time (min)
Mackerel in oil	260 X 335	125	40
Tuna in oil	160 X 242	115	40
Sardine in its own juice	150 X 200	121 °F	43

De-traying

After the stage of retorting is over it is advisable that pouches should not be handled in order to avoid contamination. All subsequent operations from de-traying to over wrapping are done automatically. Automatic de-traying equipments pick up pouches from retort trays, using vacuum suckers, transfer them to rinsing and drying equipments.

Rinsing

Rinsing is done by chlorinated water having chlorine at 10 ppm level.

This step is to prevent microbial contamination. Any scales and impurities which get attached to the pouches from retort are also removed by this rinsing.

Drying

Pouches coming out of rinsing equipment will be wet. They have to be dried before cartoning. Certain types of air knives are used to remove the bulk of the water. The internal heat of the pouch facilitates removal of the last traces of adhering water film from the surface of the pouches.

Outer Packing/Over wrapping

The purpose of using an outer carton/packaging is to prevent damages to the pouches while handling them during transit storage and retail sales in shops. It is also an additional safety for internal contents like fish etc, which otherwise are likely to get mascerated by hand while consumer handles them. Outer wraps also prevent attack by rodents. The type of outer packaging currently in use include cartons, film overwraps and lidded, semirigid thermoformings. Of these, end load, glue sealed cartons are most widely used. Now-a-days fully automatic machines are used for outer packing of the pouches.

Bulk Packing for Transport and Sale

Retort pouches are packed in corrugated master cartons for transport and sale. The size and number of pouches to be placed in a master carton will depend upon the contents. Pouches are usually packed in horizontal configuration for extra stability.

Quality Control

Maintenance of good quality control is important in retort pouch processing and all factors applicable in canning should be followed. A Good Manufacturing Practice (GMP) must be followed by each manufacturer. It is preferable to batch/code all pouches by embossing mouth seal. Following Critical Control Points (CCP) should be rigorously controlled to ensure microbial safety of pouch packs.

1. Environmental sanitation and hygiene.
2. Measurement of correct thermal processing time.
3. Control of air inside the pouch to the minimum.
4. Protection of seal area from contamination by food material.
5. Maintenance of good seal integrity.
6. Hygienic handling after retorting.

Apart from this quality of the material used to manufacture the pouch as well as the type of adhesive used for lamination are two very important factors which always require attention. Sterility of the pack must be tested before marketing as per standard testing procedure.

Sealing Defects

One of the most important defects seen for retort pouch packs is the seal defect. Integrity of seal depends on sealing temperature, distribution of temperature on the seal-bar, speed of seal, time and seal pressure. Overheating and uneven heating of the seal-bar are two common phenomena noted. To avoid this a teflon tape is usually placed over the sealing-bar surface to avoid direct contact with the plastic film.

Some typical seal defects and their description seen in retort packs

Defects	*Description/reasons*
Defective seals	Wrinkles on the width of seal and foldings of the material on seal area.
Leaks	Broken or loose seal or external damage, open pin holes.
De-shaped pouches	Due to de-lamination, use of wrong adhesives for bonding.
Bulged packs after retorting	Overfilling
Soft and hard swell	
a. Under processing	Insufficient retorting.
b. Not under processing	Due to gas formation, defective de-aeration during filling and sealing.
Punctures/cuts	Due to external action while handling.
Dirts	Smeared to surface during processing or got attached from retort.

Internal contents disintegrated and soft.	Due to over processing or pin holes in the pouch.

Retort Pouch Packing of Sardine

One popular way of preserving small pelagic fish like sardine is by canning. Canned sardines, herring and mackerel have long been commercially important. In India cost of can has limited this means of marketing this important pelagic resource of India. Packing sardine in retort pouch appears feasible and economical as pouches can be indigenously produced cheaply.

Process

Sardines are dressed and blanched in 15 per cent brine for 15 minutes. After draining the fish is packed in pouches. Sterilised gloves are used at all stages to prevent contamination. Four sardines are packed in each pouch, filling them into one layer.

Vacuum Sealing

The pouches are sealed under vacuum. Both air removal and sealing are performed by an automatic double element vacuum sealing machine. After this they are arranged in trays. The filled trays are stacked in trolleys and put into the retort for heat processing.

Heat Processing

This is done in special retort designed for retort pouch processing. This retort has provision for maintaining the overhead pressure and for water cooling under pressure. After loading the retort, the water for heating is admitted to about 10cm above the retort rack. Steam is introduced to raise the process temperature to 121°C. The overhead pressure is maintained at 25 psig. Heat processing is carried out to a lethal value Fo = 10.

Drying

After retorting the pouches are washed, cooled and dried

automatically. The pouches are then packed in individual cartons.

The whole process can be summarised as

Preformed pouches ----> Filling fish into pouches ----> Air removal ----> Sealing ----> Traying ----> Retort loading ----> Retorting ----> Retort unloading ----> Rinsing and drying ----> Outer packing.

Specifications of Pouches used for Packing Sardines

1. Length and width	:	150 x 200 mm
2. Seal size	:	10 mm
3. Lip size	:	0.5 mm (as required)
4. Notch position	:	30 mm from end
5. Notch size	:	2 mm
6. Inner appearance	:	Dark silver/grey
7. Outer appearance	:	Light silver/light grey
8. Burst pressure	:	Minimum 40 psig for 30 seconds
9. Seal strength	:	Minimum 75 N/25 mm
10. Outer laminate material and its thickness	:	Polyester film 12 micron
11. Thickness of aluminium	:	9 micron
12. Inner laminate material and its thickness	:	Polypropylene 70 micron

Results of Technical Evaluation

Sardines remained in good conditions for a period upto 3 years. No delamination was noted. Consumer preference studies conducted by test marketing, all over India, showed that over 95 per cent people rated the packs as better than canned fish and 71 per cent were ready to purchase the item if available in the market. With regard to cost of the packs 28.9 per cent desired to be cheaper than canned fish. It was concluded that Indian oil sardines (*Sardinella longiceps*), can be processed in retortable pouches to give a good quality product having shelf-life upto 3 years at ambient temperatures of India.

Standard Testing Methods for Assessment of Quality of Retort Pouches

1. *Determination of Surface Wetability*

Usually visking solutions are used for this. Apply the solution with a cotton bud (of the Johnson's type) across the whole width of the surface gently with light pressure. After 30 seconds check whether solution has not dewetted any point of the surface. Dewetting indicates that wetability of the surface is below the surface tension of the solution used. Testing must be done on fresh films only.

2. *Determination of Laminate for Product Resistance*
   Product : Any product to be packed.

   Procedure

   (i) Take two sets of pouches for control and sample. Fill 6 pouches with the product to be packed.
   Fill 6 pouches with water (control).
   (ii) Seal all the pouches at 230°C.
   (iii) Retort the samples and control in a pressure retort suitable for retort pouch processing (Toya Seikan). 30 minutes for water filled pouches and 45 minutes for fish/meat filled pouches.
   (iv) Cool to room temperature, empty the contents and wash the pouches thoroughly with cold water.
   (v) Cut the pouches into strips of 1 X 25mm size from the machine direction and another pouch in transverse direction, cutting across the seam area. Pull the seam apart and delaminate and examine the plies.
   (vi) The laminate plies can be separated apart using an Instron Universal Testing Machine or Zwick universal machine and observe the bond strength in g/25mm. Recommended cross head speed 300mm/min.

3. *Determination of Process Resistance of Pouches*

Place one crumpled and another uncrumpled pouches in a pressure cooker containing some water. Heat to 121°C (15 psig steam pressure). After 30 minutes cool and take the pouch and examine carefully for delamination. Grade delamination.

4. *Test for Burst Strength*

A burst strength measuring equipment is used. Clamp the pouch lips around the air inlet and between the rubber jaws and tight well. Release air gradually for 30 seconds. If the pouch can hold air for 30 seconds without bursting it passes the test. It also shows absence of pin holes in the pouch. For a standard pouch burst pressure must be consistantly equal or greater than 45 psig (Table 8.6).

TABLE 8.6: Specifications for standard pouches*

Items	Specifications (Recommended minimum)
Seal size (mm)	8 ± 2
Lip size (mm)	0.5 max
Notch position (mm)	25 ± 1
Notch size (mm)	2.5 ± 1
Outer appearance	No major defects
Burst pressure (psig)	40 (absolute minimum)
Seal strength (N/25mm)	75 (absolute minimum) control limit 85.
Process resistance — Outer ply	Grade 1 or 2
Inner ply	No delamination

* Specification as applicable to Meta pack-RP-F (*Courtesy:* Metal Box, UK)

5. *Determination of Seal Strength*

Heat sealability of a packaging film is one of the most important properties when considering its use on retort pouch equipment and of course, the integrity of the seal is of tremendous importance to the ultimate package. After the seal is made, the strength is determined by measuring the force required to pull apart the pieces of film which have been sealed together. The breaking strength of the heat sealed seams is determined in a universal testing machine following ASTM (1.73) F. 88-68. The specimen shall not be more than 25mm in width. The initial jaw separation shall be 50 ± 1.5mm and the seam shall be equidistant ± 1.5 mm between the two jaws. The rate of loading shall

TABLE 8.7: Properties of some commercial retort pouches

Details	Composition*	Process resistance of the retort pouches	Heat seal strength N/25mm width	
			MD	CD
Imported (Japanese)	12.5 μ PEST/25 μ Al. foil/ 12.5 μ Nylon/300g PP	No delamination	122.60	96.81
Imported (DRG Sterilite)	12.5 μ PEST/12.5 μ Al. foil/370g PP	No delamination	96.11	83.32
Imported (U.K.)	12.5 μ PEST/12.5 μ Al. foil/300g PP	No delamination	98.11	81.30
Indigenous:				
Source I	12.5 μ PEST/12.5 μ Al. foil/370g PP	No delamination	62.50	60.39
Source II	12.5 μ PEST/12.5 μ Al. foil/300g PP	No delamination	71.52	58.27

* — Measured after delamination in CIFT lab.
MD — Machine Direction
CD — Cross Direction
PEST — Polyester
PP — Polypropylene
Heat seal strength measured in ZWICK 1484 Universal Testing Machine
μ — micron

be such that the lower clamp moves at a rate of 200mm/minute. Record the maximum stress applied to the specimen at yield or breakage. Absolute minimum recommended seal strength for retort pouch is 75 N/25mm width (Table 8.7).

REFERENCE

Keith D. Jeffs: 1984: *Retort Pouch Packing Special Bulletin*, Central Institute of Fisheries Technology, Cochin, pp. 1-12.

NINE

MODIFIED ATMOSPHERE PACKAGING OF FISH AND FISHERY PRODUCTS

S.K. BHATTACHARYYA

Controlled atmosphere and modified atmosphere packagings of fresh produces like fruits and vegetables and meats have gained tremendous popularity in European countries during last thirty years and in the United States of America in the last seven years. In Denmark, 42 per cent of all retail meat is packed under modified atmosphere, followings are U.K. with 29 per cent, France with 15 per cent and Germany with 5 per cent (Lioutas, 1988). Moreover, advances in the design and manufacture of different polymeric films having high and wide ranges of gas permeabilities have created interest for modified atmosphere storage for mainly respiring foods. Over and above the availabilities of absorbers and adsorbers of oxygen, carbon dioxide, ethylene and water provide additional tools for maintaining a desired atmosphere within a package.

Modified atmosphere packaging is often wrongly termed as controlled atmosphere packaging. Modified atmosphere packaging means replacing the air in a pack with a different mixture of gases and once the proportion of each component gas is fixed, no further change in the gas mixture is exercised. In contrast, in controlled atmosphere packaging, continuous control in the gas mixture is exercised throughout the storage. The gases normally employed are carbon dioxide, mixtures of carbon dioxide and nitrogen, carbon dioxide and oxygen, and carbon dioxide, oxygen and nitrogen with the sole objective to extend the shelf-life of the product beyond that obtained in conventional refrigerated storages. Packaging materials generally employed for this purpose are flexible films of Nylon/Surlyn laminates, plastic moulded trays and over wrap with

PVC stretch film, polyester/low density polythene film, etc.

Fish being one of the most perishable foods, its freshness is rapidly lost even when stored under chilled conditions. Further, consumers wish to have fish in as fresh a state as possible so that the characteristic flavours are retained. Bulk transportation of fresh fish in ice has several limitations like limited extension of storage life, unnecessary expenditure on freight due to ice, difficulty in handling and maintaining hygienic conditions due to leaching of ice melt water with leaching losses of soluble nutrients and flavouring compounds. Modified atmosphere packaging systems have shown great potential as a valuable technological tool for handling, preservation and distribution of fresh fish. It is primarily the enrichment of carbon dioxide in the storage atmosphere as a means of controlling microbial growth which results to the extension of shelf-life of food products. There have been many studies of the effects of CO_2 on tissues and micro-organisms. Carbon dioxide lowers the intra- and extra-cellular pH of tissues and possibly that of micro-organisms. The carbon dioxide/bicarbonate ratio has been found to have appreciable effect on the permeabilities of membranes. Further, it may affect the membrane potential of micro-organisms and influence on the equilibrium of decarboxylating enzymes of micro-organisms.

Kolbe (1882) was the first to investigate and discover the preservative effect of CO_2 on meat. Coyne (1932, 1933) was one of the early workers to apply modified atmospheres to fishery products. He observed that several pure cultures of bacteria isolated from fish are inhibited by CO_2 whereas air or nitrogen atmospheres have no inhibitory effect on growth patterns of bacteria. He found that 20 to 100 per cent CO_2 atmospheres were very effective for the preservation of fresh haddock, cod, sole, whiting and plaice in the round as well as fillet forms with the optimal concentration of 40 to 50 per cent CO_2. Stansby and Griffiths (1935) found CO_2 25 per cent could double the shelf-life of the whole haddock than the conventional methods. Shewan (1950) suggested the use of 30 to 40 per cent CO_2 for the optimal benefits of modified atmosphere. Tarr (1954) made similar observation suggesting to use 50 per cent CO_2 thus advocating that the preservative effect may be negligible below 40 per cent CO_2. Yokoseki et al. (1956) observed that CO_2 atmospheres were beneficial for the storage of fish cakes. However, Haines (1933) while working with fresh meat demonstrated that concentrations of CO_2 as low as 10 to 20 per cent of the atmosphere were sufficient to inhibit effectively the growth of achromobacter (now acinetobacter, moraxella) and Pseudomonas cultures. He also found that the inhibition of CO_2 was manifested in an increased lag phase and a slower rate of growth during the logarithmic growth phase. Inhibition by CO_2 was found to be more effective when the product was stored at the lower range of refrigerated temperatures. Brown et al. (1980) looked at the feasibility of holding rockfish fillets and silver salmon steaks under MA with/without the inclusion of one per cent CO to prevent any discolouration. They found 50 per cent CO_2 was more effective in controlling undesirable chemical and microbiological changes. The inclusion of one per cent CO was somewhat effective in preventing the discoluration of rockfish fillets. It needs to be mentioned that while studying the preservation and colour stability for beef, Wolfe et al. (1976) and Gee and Brown (1978 a, b) found that one per cent carbon monoxide could be mixed with 50 per cent CO_2 atmosphere. It is believed that in the presence of CO, the carboxymyoglobin pigment is formed which is more resistant to oxidation in the presence of high levels of CO_2 than oxymyoglobin. However, as many fish and shell-fish are practically void of myoglobin, very high levels of CO_2 could be used to have the maximal bacteriostatic effect with little risk of discolouration. Fey and Regenstein (1979) found that a 60 per cent CO_2 atmosphere was very advantageous in extending the shelf-life of fresh red hake. Pretreatment by dipping in one per cent sorbate solution further extended the shelf-life of the fish. Parkin et al. (1981) reported that shelf-life of fresh rock cod fillets (*Sebastes* sp.) could be extended very effectively in MA containing 80 per cent CO_2 and 20 per cent air, Nelson and Tretsven (1975) found that gas mixture of 11.5 per cent CO_2; 1.5 per cent O_2; 87 per cent N_2 could extend the shelf-life of salmon by 4-6 days in comparison to that held in air. However, in continuous gas flow the shelf-life extension was increased by 7-9 days. The risk of growth of *C. botulinum* type E and production of its toxin can be minimised or eliminated successfully by adoption of proper refrigeration practices.

In Norway for commercial packing of cod fillets, a mixture of 50 per cent CO_2 and 50 per cent O_2 is employed. For white fish, scampi, shrimp and scallops, a mixture of 40 per cent CO_2 ; 30 per cent N_2 and 30 per cent O_2 is used. For salmon, trout and fatty fishes such as herring and mackerel a mixture of 60 per cent CO_2 and 40 per cent O_2 is practised (Srinivasa Gopal et al. 1986). Smoked salmon packed in the above mixture may show a green discolouration during storage. The extent of greening is found to be dependent on the strength of the smoke cure. In such cases, the mixture of gases recommended for white fish is to be used.

Recent work in CIFT (Srinivasa Gopal, et al. 1990) proved that a mixture of 80 per cent CO_2 and 20 per cent O_2 was more beneficial in extending the shelf-life of *Catla catla* fillets when stored at 0-4°C. The shelf-life was limited to 28 days using 80 per cent CO_2 and 20 per cent O_2, 20 days in gas mixtures of 50 per cent CO_2 and 50 per cent O_2 compared to 12 days in air. At the time of spoilage i.e. on 14 days of storage; the bacterial flora in fish stored in air was mainly *Aeromonas* (88%), *Vibrio* (3%), *Enterobacteriaceae* (3%) and *Lactobacillus* (6%). In the case of 50 per cent CO_2 and 50 per cent O_2, the bacterial flora at the time of spoilage i.e.on 22 days of storage was *Aeromonas* (63%) ; *Vibrio* (3%) ; *Enterobacteriaceae* (9%) and *Lactobacillus* (25%) whereas in the case of 80 per cent CO_2 and 20 per cent O_2, the bacterial flora of the spoiled fish on 29 days of storage was *Aeromonas* (48%), *Vibrio* (5%), *Pseudomonas* (9%) ; *Bacillus* (5%) and *Lactobacillus* (33%).

Currently modified atmosphere packing is said to cost twice the cost of vacuum packing and for continuous production of rigid packs, expensive packaging machineries and thermoformable films are required. Moreover, modified atmosphere packs being two or three times bulkier than normal packs, it makes transportation and storage costlier. There also remains a risk of wall-collapse when high proportions of carbon dioxide are used due to its high solubility in fish tissue. Wet fish products in MA are likely to exude drip for which a pad of absorbent paper can be laid inside the pack. Packs with faulty seals can be checked by pressing them with hands. Faulty packs will collapse.

Simpler and cheaper machines can be used for modified atmosphere packing where the machines pack the products in flexible bags or on trays inside bag to form what is known as a pillow pack. Sophisticated machines which continously form packs with rigid bases from rolls of thermoformable plastic films are more expensive and can produce at a rate of more than thirty a minute. In such cases, the designs of packaging films with low gas permeability must be made according to the machine maker's specification. There are, however, some machines which can be used for both modified atmosphere packing as well as for vacuum packing.

The use of modified atmospheres for the storage and transport of fish seems to have great potential. Although considerable work needs to be done to know the ideal conditions for modified atmosphere storage of different fishes of different seasons, it will be worthwhile to develop this technology further.

REFERENCES

Brown, W.D., Albright, M., Watts, D.A., Heyer, B., Spruce, B. and Price, R.J. 1980: Modified atmosphere storage on rockfish (Sebastes miniatus) and silver salmon (Oncorhynchus kisutch) *J. Food Sci.* 45, 93-96

Coyne, F.P. 1932: The effect of carbon dioxide on bacterial growth with special reference to the preservation of fish I. *J. Soc. Chem. Ind.* 51, 119T-121T

Coyne, F.P. 1933: The effect of carbon dioxide on bacterial growth with special reference to the preservation of fish II. *J. Soc. Chem. Ind.* 52, 19T-24T

Fey, M. and Regenstein, J.M. 1979: Shelf-life extension of fresh fish. Presented at the Atlantic Fisheries Technological Conference, Danvers. M.A

Gee, D.L. and Brown, W.D. 1978a: Stability of carboxymyoglobin in refrigerated ground beef *J. Agric. Food Chem.* 26, 273-274

Gee, D.L. and Brown, W.D. 1978b: Extension of shelf-life in refrigerated ground beef stored under an atmosphere containing carbon dioxide and carbon monoxide. *J. Agric. Food Chem.* 26, 274-276

Haines, R.B. 1933: The influence of carbon dioxide on the rate of multiplication of certain bacteria, as judged by viable counts *J. Soc. Ind. Chem.* 52, 13T-17T

Kolbe, H. 1882: Antiseptiche eigneschaften der Kohlensaure. *J.Prakt. Chem.* 26, 249-255

Lioutas, T.S. 1988: Challenges of controlled and modified atmosphere packaging : A Food Company's Perspective, *Food Technology*, 42, 79

Nelson, R.W. and Tretsven, W.I. 1975: Storage of Pacific salmon in controlled atmosphere. Proc. XIVth Int. Congress on Refrigeration, Moscow, U.S.S.R.

Parkin, K.L., Wells, M.J. and Brown, W.D. 1981: Modified Atmosphere Storage of Rockfish Fillets. *J. Food. Sci.* 47, 181-183

Shewan, J.M. 1950: Improving the quality of white fish by the use of gas storage. *Fish News.* 1946, 14-15

Srinivasa Gopal, T.K., Nambiar, V.N., Bhattacharyya, S.K., Joseph Jose and Prabhu, P.V. 1990: Modified atmosphere storage of fresh water fish fillets (*Catla catla*). Presented at the meeting of International Institute of Refrigeration on "Chilling and freezing of new fish products", *Aberdeen*, 18-20th Sept., 1990

Srinivasa Gopal, T.K., Rao, C.V.N. and Govindan, T.K. 1986: Packaging of Fish in Modified Atmospheres in Packaging of Food Products Publ. Indian Institute of Packaging, 99-100

Stansby, M.E. and Griffiths, F.P. 1935: Carbon dioxide in handling fresh fish. Ind. *Eng. Chem.* 27, 1452-1458

Tarr, H.L.A. 1954: Microbiological deterioration of fish postmortem, its detection and control. *Bacteriol. Rev.* 18, 1-5

Wolfe, S.K., Brown, W.D. and Silliker, J.H. 1976: Transfresh shipping of meat. *Proc. Meat. Ind. Res. Conf.* Chicago, pp. 137-148

Yokoseki, M., Uchiyama, H. and Amano, K. 1956: Preservation of fish cakes IV. Factors involved in preservative effect of carbon dioxide. *Bull Jpn. Soc. Sci. Fish.* 22, 35-40

TEN

PLASTIC CORRUGATED BOARD IN PACKAGINGS

M/S CAPRIHANS (INDIA) LTD., BOMBAY

Introduction

Hollow Plastic Corrugated Board also known as Cellular Profile Board was introduced in India in 1981 as a complimentary packaging material to paper board and wood materials. Essentially the Plastic Corrugated Board (PCB) is a one piece extrusion consisting of two flat layers or skins separated by vertical ribbing with the thickness varying between 0.4 mm and 0.8 mm with an interspace of 4 mm. The material used is generally HDPE or a polypropylene copolymer and currently acrylic and polycarbonate are very popular abroad for nonpackaging applications especially in construction and buildings. Another profile design instead of vertical ribbing is also commercially available abroad though not yet in India.

Plastic corrugated board is now manufactured in India by Caprihans India Limited. The sheet thicknesses are available in 1.5 mm, 2 mm, 3 mm, 5 mm and 6 mm with an average weight varying from 400 gm to 1200 gm. The board is extruded in widths ranging from 1.30 to 1.35 mtrs and cut off lengths can be upto 3 mtrs. maximum. The rigid board so produced is tough, light in weight and can be cut, folded, glued, stiched and welded.

It's high strength/weight ratio and good cushioning properties coupled with durability and ability to recover well after rough handling make it an ideal material for multi-trip/ multi-usage application.

The Need

In the Indian context there is a most pressing need on the national front to conserve our natural resources of wood and not to allow them to be used in the least profitable manner viz. packaging as well as to develop alternative, more economical and better materials. In our country generally plastics are more expensive than any natural material viz. wood or paper board etc. Hence very often the cost of a design made from plastic corrugated board is more expensive than that of a comparative corrugated paper box or a wooden box. The prime reason for higher cost is import duties and the excise duties which are levied on the basic material.

The purpose of this note is to demonstrate and highlight the fact that inspite of this apparent higher cost, economics can be gained by the use of this material in the long run.

Features and Advantages

(a) *High strength:* High rigidity, excellent edge crush strength, puncture strength and superior dimensional stability, excellent compression strength.

(b) *Low weight:* Weight reduction by 50 per cent to 300 per cent compared to equivalent corrugated board or wooden box. Freight saving for air freighters. Easy to handle, less cumbersome than wood.

(c) *Superior safety and protection:* Offers superior packaging protection due to excellent burst strength, puncture resistance, rigidity, as compared to corrugated board and wood. Suitably designed boxes can also replace thermocole as it has excellent cushioning property and offers drop protection.

(d) *Protection from environment:* PCB is waterproof, chemical proof and vermin proof. Can be kept outdoors. Ideal for garment/leather exports.

(e) *Attractive packaging:* Specially for consumer goods where attractively designed packages can increase product appeal by offering a usable box. PCB comes in attractive bright colours.

(f) *Durability/Multitrip applications:* Because of high hinge strength and stiffness compared to paper board boxes it can take 7 to 10 or more returns. Ideal for material handling as it weighs much less than wooden box.

(g) *Cleanability:* Easily cleanable by water, steam, soap etc. Ideal for products where packing can be sterilised along with product.

(h) *Printability:* Excellent and attractive screen printing can be done. Ideal for hoardings, display signs, show window signs, greeting cards, etc.

(i) *Easy processability:* PCB can easily be cut by scissors, folded, creased, stapled, pressed, riveted, punched. Boxes can be made on the same machine which processes corrugated paper board boxes.

(j) *Translucent/opaque colours:* Translucent PCB can be used to replace or cut labels visible inside the box.

(k) *Long Life:* Can be stored outdoors either in the form of boxes or temporary shelters, roofing garage. Does not decay or rot with time.

(l) *Non Toxic*: Suitable for food packing.

(m) *Insulation:* PCB offers good sound and thermal insulation properties.

Fabrication

For manufacture of PCB boxes, same machinery which is used for paper board boxes application can be used. Joints can be made by the method of stapling, riveting or sticking with a tape. It can also be glued with solvent paste as well as hot melt adhesive of a very good quality though such glue is not yet available in India. Another method of sealing is ultrasonic welding. Such machines are to be imported. Currently the most common system in use is stapling and riveting using the same machines required for paper board boxes.

Printing and Decoration

Plastic Corrugated Board (PCB) is available in bright opaque colours viz. yellow, blue, orange, green, brown, etc. and also in natural, clear and other translucent shades. These bright colours provide aesthetic appeal and can also be used to colour code the products.

The product is automatically electrically pre-treated on both surface when it is manufactured which makes it suitable for silk screen printing. Attractive multi colour printing can be done and this is the most widely used printing method upto date. Suitable inks are available from the printing ink manufacturers and normal air drying is used. If an oven is used for drying, the temperature should be kept below 55°C as the sheet is softened above this temperature. It is recommended that whenever possible the squeegee should be drained across the flutes rather than down the length.

Letter press and flexographic techniques have been used abroad for printing with limited success and are not very popular yet. In India there are many screen printers who are also doing printing on this material.

Application

PCB is a unique material because of its extremely wide range of possible applications in both packaging and non-packaging areas. For non-packaging areas it can be used for construction industries in interior decoration, display stands, advertising materials, files, folders, toys, novelties and many others. Here we will concentrate on the packaging applications and see where PCB can be of use to us.

Packaging Applications

Agricultural products viz. apples, mangoes, tea, tobacco, fresh vegetables, etc.

Timber is now extensively used for making packages for tea, fruits and tobacco. For fruits around 200 million wooden cases are required and another 100 million plywood cases for tea. The total timber requirement has been estimated to 55.5 lakh cubic feet per year. This naturally leads to large cutting of our forests and its consequential effects on the ecology and the environment are expected to be drastic. If this requirement is not cut down, the forest resources will soon be depleted beyond a critical level causing irreparable damage to our ecology.

PCB can be used for these applications especially for apples and fruits and a mechanism needs to be worked out by which these boxes can be collected back from the dealers to the farms and the same boxes can be used five to six times thereby bringing out tremendous savings to the overall economy.

The biggest constraint in the introduction of PCB in this area has been that there is a resistance to get involved in the system requiring return of such containers.

Unit Packaging

A unit packing box made of PCB will offer the advantages of a novel look to the product and make it look more attractive. PCB can be used to offer a usable box suitably designed for consumer specially in consumer products.

This is an ideal material available to an innovative marketing man who would like to identify the product separately from many others in case of competition. The product is given better protection in a PCB box.

In suitably designed boxes, use of thermocole may also be avoided by giving proper ribs made out of this material, thereby giving cost savings.

Thus in case of consumer oriented goods, a PCB usable plastic box will offer an attraction to consumer and because of better aesthetics and protection, higher sales could be achieved.

Bulk Packing

PCB gives good protection and can be used for making bulk cartons to replace paper boards and wooden boxes. The major advantage is ease of handling and lighter weight specially for exporters who have to air freight their consignments as in case of leather goods and garments. They will get an overall economy because of protection and lower freight charges.

Because of its inherent high strength, PCB boxes can take multiple returns. Therefore, units supplying goods to dealers can get a substantial cost saving if they can arrange to get the boxes back and reuse them. Properly handled, these boxes may last 7 to 10 times compared to one or two of paper board boxes. The bringing back cost will be marginal as these can be collapsed which is not possible in case of wooden boxes.

The goods which need to be kept exposed to rain, sunshine or adverse weather, will get the best protection in PCB boxes.

Cost Comparisons

Given below is some cost comparisons between wooden boxes,

corrugated paper boxes and PCB boxes.

For example, a 50 kgs. tea chest weighing around 6.1 kgs. cost approximately Rs. 35 compared to an equivalent paper corrugated box of 3.8 kgs. costing approximately Rs. 60 and an equivalent 1.5 kgs. box of PCB costs about Rs. 55. In case of export, a further duty drawback of approximately Rs. 5 will be available on PCB boxes.

Another example can be given of an organisation exporting small drills to U.S.A. and paying air freight charges of Rs. 35 per kg. Present packing cost is Rs. 8 for a paper board box weighing 650 gms and Rs. 23 towards freight making total cost Rs. 31 per kg. Compared to this equivalent PCB will cost Rs.16 and air freight will be Rs. 9.50 as the box will weigh only 270 gms. thus making a net advantage of Rs. 5.50 per box.

Even if it is assumed that the above boxes used locally are recycled 3 to 5 times, the average cost will come down from Rs. 16 to Rs. 3 per box.

In case of unit packages for beautification of a product the additional cost of packing will result in higher sales and better market shares.

Summary

The introduction of PCB in the Indian Market has met with success in the following industries:

Electronics, Mixy, Electric irons, Automobile parts, Utensils, Medicines, Sophisticated instruments, Photographic instruments and in material bending application.

It is being increasingly used for innovative marketing effort for making a product more attractive. Many buyers today are increasingly getting concerned at the use of wood in packaging and have started trying out PCB for replacing wooden boxes. A few leading companies are also trying to establish the concept of returnable cartons which will give them substantial cost savings.

Specifications of PCB

A. *Availability*

Thickness	*Standard sheet weight*
1.5 mm	410 gsm

2.0 mm	440 gsm
3.0 mm	500 gsm
4.0 mm	635 gsm
5.0 mm	770 gsm

Other thicknesses and weights are available depending upon the requirements.

Standard size

Normal width	1.3 mtrs. (maximum)
Normal length	2 mtrs. (maximum upto 3 m)

It is possible to manufacture sheets in longer lengths subject to certain conditions.

B. *Flute Direction*

It is important to identify the flute direction in order that the material supplied meets the end use requirement.

C. *Colours*

Available in Opaque: Blue, Black, White, Brown, Red, Orange, Yellow and Green.
Available in Translucent : Clear, Green and Red.

D. *Surface Treatment*

Sheets are "Corona" treated for printing purpose.

E. *Flammability/Fire Precautions*

Like other organic polymers, polypropylene will burn. It is combustible but not highly inflammable.

Flame retardant grades are available for specific uses. The product is non-toxic and the products of combustion are carbon dioxide, sunpac sheet carbon monoxide.

F. *PCB Specifications*

Sl. No.	Properties	Units	Thickness			
			2mm	3mm	4mm	5mm
1.	Grammage	gms/sq.m.	440	500	635	770
2.	Puncture Resistance	OZS/INCH	335	–	632	698
3.	Bursting strength	kg/sq.cm	12.2	–	does not burst	
4.	Edge Crush	kg/10cms	65	71	95.7	114
5.	Load bearing capacity for boxes (compression)					
	a) 60 X 40 X 50 cms		–	–	298	466
	b) 54 X 23 X 36 cms		–	–	221	300
	c) 46 X 33 X 46 cms		–	137	200	280

G. *Material properties of resin used for the production of PCB*

Property	ASTM test	Units	Values
Melt index	D 1238 - 65T Cond.L	6/10 min	0.75
Tensile strength	D 638 – 67T	kg/cms	285
Elongation at break	D 638 – 67T	Per cent	200
Stiffness (Flexural)	D747-63	kg/sq.cm.	1200
Tensile strength (at yield)	D638-67	kg/sq.cm.	285
Hardness rockwell (L scale)	D785-63	–	58

H. *Other properties*

Property	ASTM test	Units	Values
Normal density	ASTM D 1505	gm/sq.cm.	0.905
Softening point	BS 2782:102D	°C	145
Brittle point	D 746-64T	°C	-35
Water absorption (unpigmented)	ASTM-D-570	%	–0.02

I. *Chemical Resistance*

A. *Organic Reagent*	Temperature	
	20°C	60°C
Acetic acid (10%)	Nil	Nil
Acetone	Nil	Nil
Ammonium hydroxide (10%)	Nil	Nil
Benzene	Slight	Moderate
Carbon Tetrachloride	Moderate	Severe

Citric acid (10%)	Nil	Nil
Cyclohexanol	Nil	Slight
Detergent (2% liquid)	Nil	Nil
Ethanol (96%)	Nil	Nil
Glycerine	Nil	Nil
Isopropyl Alcohol	Nil	Nil
Lactic acid (20%)	Nil	Nil
Methanol	Nil	Nil
Methyl Ethyl Ketone	Nil	Slight
Nitrobenzene	Nil	Nil
Turpentine	Slight	Moderate
Xylene	Moderate	Severe
B. *Inorganic*		
Hydrochloric acid (30%)	Nil	Nil
Hydrogen peroxide (10%)	Nil	Slight
Nitric acid (10%)	Nil	Nil
Nitric acid (70%)	Slight	Moderate
Sulphuric acid (98%)	Nil	Moderate
Sulphuric acid (10%)	Nil	Nil
Phosphoric acid	Nil	Nil
Potassium hydroxide (50%)	Nil	Nil
Water	Nil	Nil

Corrugated Plastic Board for Fish Packaging

Light weight containers having capacities of 20 kg. and 40 kg. of iced fish were fabricated from 5 mm. thick corrugated polypropylene boards with 2 cm. thick expanded polystyrene slab enclosed in 300 gauge polyethylene sleeving with nylon rope handles (Fig. 10.1). Fresh jew fish was chilled in crushed ice for 4 hours prior to packaging in the boxes to bring down its temperature to 2°C or below. Fish and ice 1:1 were packed to a density 1200 kg/cu.m in alternate layers, each layer not exceeding 7.5 cm to effect equitable temperature distribution. The container was kept in shade at ambient temperature (23 to 32°C). The quality of fish judged organoleptically at regular intervals showed it to be in marketable fresh condition for 48 to 56 hours. Mean temperature at the end of the storage was 4°C.

It is reusable for 5 trips and being of collapsible design and light weight return of empties is very much cheaper. The cost of fabrication of the box including PP board, polythene film and foamed polystyrene slab works out to be Rs.150 to 200 depending upon the size of the box.

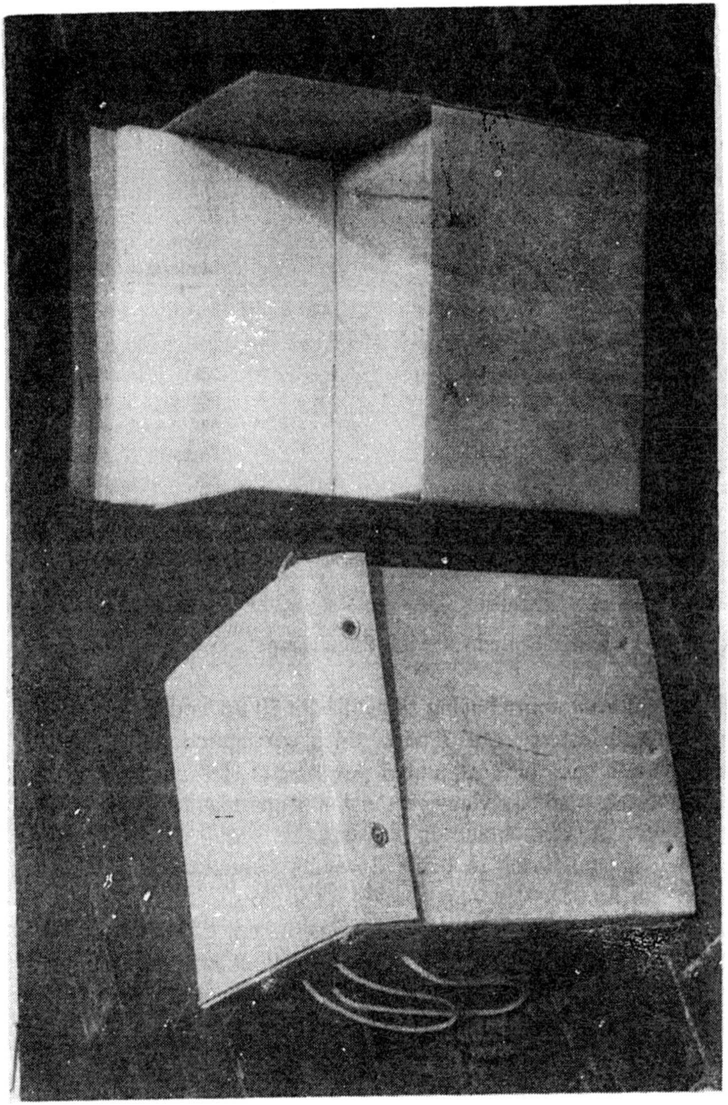

FIG 10.1: Corrugated Polypropylene board 20 kg and 40 kg capacity for fresh fish transportation developed by C.I.F.T.

Specification of the polypropylene board and box used for fish packagings

1. Grammage	:	725 gm/sq.m.
2. Caliper	:	5 mm
3. No. of corrugation	:	54/30 cm
4. Puncture resistance	:	730 beach units
5. Bursting strength (Maximum failure)	:	1.96 mpa.
6. Flat crush	:	54 N/sq.cm.

Dimension of box (External)

41 cm X 41 cm X 46 cm (L X B X H)
40 kg capacity
46 cm X 41 cm X 31 cm (L X B X H)
20 kg. capacity.
Tare weight of container.
1.5 kg to 2 kg. (20 kg and 40 kg)
Heat leakages : 0.63 K cal/Hour/°C/sq.m.

REFERENCE

Rao, C.V.N. and Antony, K.P. 1989: A multipurpose light weight container for transport of fresh iced fish. *Packaging India*, Vol. 22 No.1. April-May, pp.21-22.

ELEVEN

CORRUGATED FIBRE BOARD BOXES : QUALITY CONTROL

N.X. GEORGE

In our modern world corrugated fibre boards and boxes are being used for a wide variety of packaging needs. Corrugated boxes have become the largest used packing material.

Corrugated paper board consists of two structural components namely, the liner and the fluting media. These are, in required numbers, joined together with special adhesives. Corrugated boxes, though simple in appearance, are formed with the help of a combination of technical skills like engineering, design and graphics and hazard and transportation analysis.

Effective changes in components, design, etc. enables the corrugated box to successfully perform its various functions. Some of the important functions are, protection, storage, transportation, identification and advertising of the content.

Quality Control, General

Quality control has become an indispensible tool in modern management. Quality is not an accident. It is the result of intelligent planning. The most important point is the will to produce a superior thing. Quality Assurance (QA) needs a Good Manufacturing Practice (GMP).

In the present day world of ever changing production and marketing patterns higher quality standards alone will help a product to succeed in the competitive market. From the selection of raw materials to the finished product the entire chain of functions have to be effectively linked to thorough quality analysis. The entire process must be strategically divided into different stages and the quality must be checked at each stage.

There must be a continuing relationship between the quality tests in the laboratory and field performance of the product. The lab test must be simple to perform and must be easy to correlate with the field performance of the product.

There are three main stages of quality control namely (1) quality control on raw materials, (2) quality control in the processing stages, and (3) quality control on finished product. None of these three stages can be neglected.

Quality on finished product depends on the control exercised in the preceding stages. Quality control test on the finished product may only reveal whether quality control was successfully carried out during the earlier stages.

Approach to Quality Control on Corrugated Fibre Board

The major achievement to be derived from quality control is to correctly predict the performance of the box in various situations and to provide it with necessary strength. Quality control is the most significant factor for the total performance of the package.

Some of the hazards the corrugated cases may face are:-

1. *Crushing*: Stacking, and shifting of load in transit can cause this problem.
2. *Impact or Shock*: Due to dropping, throwing, etc.
3. *Vibration*: Causes loosening and rubbing.
4. *Puncture*: Outside contact with projectiles results in punctured surface.
5. *Water/Moisture*: Exposure to rain and due to condensation on removal from deep-freeze; humidity conditions in stores or in transit.
6. *Contamination*: Penetration or contamination by foreign substances from surroundings like gases or insects.
7. *Temperature change*: Movement from hot to cold or vice-versa.
8. *Misplacement*: Can get misplaced in transit or in stores.
9. *Pilferage*: Theft of whole package or portion of contents.

As already stated total quality control must start from the quality control analysis on raw materials.

Since the basic component of the corrugated box is the kraft paper it is essential to have quality control analysis on this material. Equally important is the adhesive.

The standard quality checks on kraft paper are as follows:

1. *Shade* : The shade should be pleasing, and that of liner should be suitable for printing.
2. *Cleanliness* : The paper should be free from dirt and excessive shives.
3. *Porosity* : Paper is a porous film. It is generally measured as the resistance of paper to the passage on air. Porosity is reported as the number of seconds required for displacing 100 ml of air. Porosity affects the absorption of adhesive and moisture.
4. *Stiffness* : Stiffness is the rigidity of paper. It is related to caliper, fibre strength, etc. Stiffness is important because the utility of a box partly depends upon its ability to resist bulging in filled condition. The stiffness of paper can be measured under the ring-stiffness or ring crush test.
5. *The uniform basis weight* : This is achieved by the uniform spread of pulp.
6. *Bursting strength* : Bursting strength is a complex function of tensile strength and stretch. Also bursting strength reveals the interfibre bonding and the pulp formation.
7. *Uniform caliper* : The paper should have uniform thickness.
8. *Stretch* : Stretch is the amount of distortion which paper undergoes under tensile stress. Stretch is a factor in the bursting strength and initial tearing resistance of paper. Also it is an important factor in the folding endurance.
9. *Tensile strength* : When corrugated board is manufactured a high tensile strength helps in resisting web breaks.

The chemical properties of paper are also very important. This directly affects the physical and other properties. Some of the chemical properties to be checked are:

1. *Moisture content* : Moisture content in paper affects its physical strength and flexibility. It also affects weight,

dimensional stability, rigidity, tearing strength, tensile strength, folding endurance and elasticity.

2. *pH* : High pH value adversely affects printing. Low pH would accelerate corrosion. pH also affects bursting strength of the paper.
3. *Sizing* : Chemical agents are used for sizing while manufacturing of paper. Some of them affects the absorption of adhesives. They also may react with adhesives when board is made.
4. *Cobb test* : Cobb test is the test carried out to measure the water absorption of paper. Cobb value reflects the sizing and similar properties.
5. *Ash content* : Low ash content is essential for high strength in paper. High ash from the residual chemicals left over from bleaching and/or dyeing are harmful to the strength and performance of paper.

Adhesives

There are many types of adhesives, but in fibre board industry the most widely used are, starch-based and sodium silicate. Some of these are available as ready mix liquid, as powder to be mixed with water, as powder to be cooked after mixing with water or gel. Following are some of the properties to be checked for the purpose of quality control on adhesives:

1. *Tackiness* : Tackiness refers to the stickiness of the adhesive. It is a combination of plasticity, adhesion and cohesion. There is no specific method to measure tackiness. The practical method is the finger test by which an experienced person gets the indication. Modern synthetic and even some starch based glues are far better in bonding strength with little or no tackiness and so in these cases tackiness is not an essential test.
2. *Viscosity* : The viscosity of an adhesive must fall within certain limit. The viscosity directs the amount of adhesive transferred through the glue roll on to the paper. Viscosity is measured by viscometer. This test is replaced by consistency test for the laboratory purpose.
3. *pH* : pH in adhesive affects the pH of the combined board.

The use of highly alkaline adhesives should be avoided, especially for the outer liner since it affects the printing.

4. *Solid content* : Solid content is another important point while selecting the adhesive. Solid content in the adhesive affects bond strength, setting time and stiffness.

Quality Control in Processing Stages

During the manufacture of Corrugated Fibre Board (CFB) different factors must be carefully checked to produce good quality board. The poor quality of CFB results in unsatisfactory functional characteristics in containers.

The quality control tests in processing are mostly non-destructive and hence could be carried out on a continuous basis. The following are some of the defects that may occur during conversion.

1. *Liner and medium not properly aligned* : This defect occurs when the webs are not properly aligned on reelstands and on the rolls. This results in wastage and naked flutes.
2. *Corrugation leaning* : Leaning corrugation is responsible for poor flat crush and poor cushioning ability.
3. *Blisters* : Due to variable viscosity of adhesives or due to too much heat or speed, the bonding would be intermittent. It affects the bursting strength, flat crush and edge values of the board.
4. *Spotty application pattern of adhesives* : This defect occurs when the adhesive is not of proper quality or the transfer roll is defective.
5. *Low formation of flutes* : Lack of appropriate moisture content or low pressure on corrugating rolls, can result in low flutes in corrugated board. Also flute rolls must be checked for wear and tear. The finished board will fail in flat crush and edge crush.

Quality Control of Finished Products

Corrugated Boards/Boxes

The usual tests conducted on corrugated board and boxes are, bursting strength, flat crush (for 3 ply board only), puncture resistance, edge crush test, bending stiffness test, pin adhesion (Liner adhesion), water resistance of glue bond, vibration test, compression strength, print quality and the strength of manufacturer's joint. These tests are carried out to ensure production of CFBs with specified quality standards.

Bending Stiffness Test

It gives the resistance of the board against bending in the selected area. However, it is not related to the buckling resistance or ultimate failure of the board or box. It is useful to test the strength of bends in boxes.

Puncture Resistance Test

The PR value represents the energy necessary for penetrating the board by a pointed head. It is a physical property and gives an idea of the required material strength to withstand an instantaneous application of force. It is dependent both on the basic materials and construction.

Pin Adhesion (Liner Adhesion)

It is the minimum force per unit length of a glued tip, necessary for separating the adhesive bond between the liner and fluting under the prescribed conditions. This test reveals the quality of adhesion which if not satisfactory, would result in delamination of substrates.

Bursting Strength Test

It is defined as the peak pressure developed in a hydraulic or pneumatic system in forcing a rubber diaphram through a circular area of a board or paper under specific conditions. It is a physical property and gives the idea of the material. It is easy to understand and record and so is adopted as a standard and common quality control test for paper and board. The bursting strength property depends on the basic material and its construction. The moisture content in the board has a direct bearing on bursting strength and with increasing moisture content the bursting strength decreases.

Vibration Test

This test helps to determine the ability of the box, including the inner fitments as well as the means of closure adopted to withstand given vibrations. It becomes more significant when sensitive products are packed inside the box.

Water Resistance of Glue Bond

The bond developed between the fluting and the liner should have adequate resistance to water or humidity conditions to avoid easy delamination. Also the outer liner especially must not get easily damaged by an unexpected shower of rain.

Compression Strength

This test gives the measure in terms of stackability of the box both under dynamic and static conditions. Compression strength is influenced by all the component materials in the box and the complete manufacturing practice. Almost all aspects that make a box directly influence the value of compression strength. For example, substance and stiffness of the liner and the corrugating medium, formation and type of corrugation, combination of corrugations, quantity and uniformity of bonding medium, bonding nature between the liner and the corrugating medium, combinations of plies, bending stiffness of the board, cutting and creasing of the board, moisture content, style of the box as well as the inner fitments all have a tangible influence on the compression strength.

The compression strength is measured under standard conditions of temperature and humidity using a universal compression strength tester with the platten movement fixed at a given speed. The compression strength comes from the load carrying capacity of the vertical panels. The load is generally concentrated only at the corners. The box fails when the lateral bulge becomes sufficiently large and failure lines transmit into the centre of the panel usually beginning from the corners. When flutes run vertically in the direction of the stacking the box will have better load carrying capacity. For combinations it is better that the heavier liner may be placed inside. For superior compression strength it should be ensured that the flutes are not crushed during conversion or printing and the ventilation holes if any must be punched away from the areas of higher stress.

As given above, the compression strength measures the load at which the board collapses under laboratory conditions. Such values are generally higher than the load when the box is stacked under sustained load in a warehouse. Therefore, such practical working load in the warehouse have to be related to the lab compression strength by a safety factor. This safety factor would be necessarily influenced by the method of stacking, storage time, moisture, etc. It can generally vary between 2 and 5.

Strength of Manufacturer's Joint

Manufacturer's joint in a box can either be stitched with suitable wire or laminated with tapes. Stitching would ensure a total grip on all plies while taping gives contact only on outer liners. For heavy duty cartons stitching with steel wires would be better. The wire must be rust proof. Number of stitches would depend on the height of the box, weight and nature of the content.

Print Quality

CFBs have become very important as an advertisement medium. Multicoloured beautifully printed boxes are an attraction on any supermarket shelf. Whether it is heavy duty boxes or carry-pack mono cartons, printed display has a very valuable role. It also helps in identification. Another important point is that probably it is the cheapest advertisement medium. So the quality of the printing must be ensured to withstand transit hazards and must be legible and appealing until the box safely and satisfactorily reaches the consumer.

(Author is *indebted* to : (a) the All India Corrugated Box Manufacturer's Association, (b) Indian Institute of Packaging, (c) Various Journals and Books on Packaging and (d) Technical Experts on Packaging).

TWELVE

PACKAGING AND TRANSPORTATION OF FRESH FISH: PRESENT STATUS

P.V. PRABHU

Transportation of any commodity in space and time is important, not only in stabilising the price line, but also in its even distribution. Fresh fish also requires careful handling and transportation. The fish landed on beaches or near lakes and reservoirs has to reach the consumers in the hinter land and far away places from the landing centres. The price of fish is generally many fold higher than the average price of many other food products and to prevent waste, even distribution by transportation and marketing becomes very essential. At present about 2.25 tonnes of marine and 1.4 tonnes of fresh water fish are being annually landed in India and about 70 per cent of the fish is consumed in fresh condition. It was about 47 per cent of the total landings being consumed in fresh condition in 1960. The phenominal increase in the fresh fish consumption has been possible due to adoption of better preservation, packaging and transport methods. Although we have achieved such progress in the distribution of fresh fish, there is large scope to further improve the packing and transport operations taking into consideration the hygienic and preservatioin aspects.

There are at least four important factors to be reckoned with when transportation of fresh fish is discussed. They are:

1. Method of preservation of fresh fish
2. Mode of transport
3. Containers for packing
4. Organisational/socio-economic factor

Method of Preservation

The fresh fish generally spoils quickly at room temperature and therefore has to be utilised or consumed within 8 hrs. of its catch if not properly preserved. There are various methods of preservation of fresh fish. However, chilling is the method universally accepted for short term preservation of fresh fish for human consumption. The chemical preservatives, though effective, are not employed for preserving fresh fish meant for human consumption. In India chilling with ice is extensively used to prolong the shelf-life of fresh fish. The price of ice is relatively low and cooling efficiency is very good. The shelf-life of fresh fish in iced temperature has been estimated to be 4 to 14 days depending on the species. The oily fishes like sardine can be kept in acceptable condition in ice only for about 3 to 4 days while prawns and lean fishes can be kept for about 2 weeks in good condition.

It is estimated that to bring down the temperature of fish from 30°C to 0°C, one kilogram of ice will be required for three kilogram of fish. Although theoretically this is correct in practice at least half kilogram of ice will have to be used for every kilogram of fish to chill the fish. Generally to chill the fish and to preserve the fish at low temperature for a reasonable period equal quantities of fish and ice are packed in suitable containers. The length of time the fish can be kept in good condition varies with the type of container used for packing as the meltage of ice depends on the insulation property of the container.

Mode of Transportation and Carriers Used

Generally fish is transported from the place of landing to processing centres, markets and consumers either by road or by rail. For facilitating transport by road/rail the primary requirement is provision of approach road to the fish landing centres which are scattered all over the coast. The vast improvements made in the distribution of fresh fish in Kerala is largely due to the provision of approach roads to the landing centres and establishment of ice plants nearby.

The physical flow of fish for domestic trade indicates, that about 50 per cent of the catches is consumed within a distance of 40 km, another 45 per cent within 200 km and balance 5 per cent beyond 200 km from the coast line. In general, in the maritime states, about 87.5 per cent of the catch is consumed within the state and interstate flow is only 12.5 per cent. For short distances by and large road transport is resorted to. Though transportation by road is costlier, this happens to be the mode of transport for fresh fish upto 200 km or even beyond as it is quicker than rail transport. About 80 per cent of the fish transported within the state is by road while only 55 per cent of interstate transport is by road. Transportation of fresh fish by road has become very significant and it has enabled the industry to distribute fresh fish to hinter land thus reducing the waste considerably.

Fish is also transported by rail to distant destinations. As perishable goods concessional tarrifs are charged for fish transported by rail. About 20 per cent of fish transport within the state and 45 per cent of interstate fish transport is by rail. Though cheaper, there are difficulties to send the consignments by rail and the time taken is invariably longer. Refrigerated wagons were introduced in several routes for taking the consignments of fish by rail. However, many of these have been suspended later as not economical. But even now large consignments of iced fish packed in suitable containers are being sent by rail from Bombay to New Delhi and Calcutta, from Coimbatore to Madras and Calcutta, etc. If properly organised this mode of transport of fish will be a boon to the traders as well as consumers of fish.

Transport of fresh fish by air is not common within the country and so the quantity of fish transported by air is scanty. The air freight is enormously high. The packaging for air transport of fish can be light and simple as the time taken is very short. Requirement of ice also can be minimised. At one time the cost of transporting one kilogram of fish by air to Bombay and New Delhi from Cochin was around Rs.9 and Rs.16 respectively while to send the same by rail was Rs. 3 and Rs.5 respectively.

Open lorries covered with tarpaulin, insulated/refrigerated trucks and tempo vans are used for long distance transport of fresh fish by road, while hand carts, bullock carts, bicycles, etc. are used for short distances.

Recently Marine Product Export Development Authority introduced insulated galvanised iron boxes for multipurpose use on boats and processing centres, of capacity 40 kg and costing Rs.700 at current rates. They are supplied at 50 per cent subsidy to the trade.

They have not become popular with the trade, in view of high tare weight (27 kgs), corrosion of metal parts in sea atmosphere etc.

The greatest disadvantage of the traditional transport packages is that with normal 1:1 ice fish ratio, they are capable of keeping fish in fair to good condition only upto a maximum period of 20 hours and are suitable for a journey of 500 to 700 km, unless steps are taken to replenish ice enroute. They have poor insulation value thus affecting the rate of melting of ice considerably.

Containers for Packing Fish for Transportation

The fish has to be packed neatly with ice in suitable containers for transportation. Designing and development of suitable containers for packing fish has been a very difficult task due to various reasons. The fish whether iced or dried is considered as a dirty cargo. Fresh fish is wet and liquid will be oozing out from the fish. Even very fresh fish has bad smell and the slime will give stinking smell. Ice in the iced fish will melt and the ice melt water has to be let out as otherwise the fish will get adversely affected. All these points have to be taken into consideration when containers for packing fish have to be developed. So far no ideal containers have been developed although improved containers are now available for fresh fish packing.

Baskets have been the traditional containers used for fresh fish transportation. They are still used largely by the trade. Baskets made of split bamboo, harhar, palmirah leaf mattings, etc. are employed to pack fish for transportation. They are more popular in Southern States. Bamboo baskets are cheap and clean when new, disposable, single service type containers. There are baskets of various shapes and sizes which can hold 40 to 100 kg of fish. Accordingly the cost of these baskets also varies from Rs.10 to Rs.25 or more. Some times these baskets are given a gunny lining all around after packing the fish, which gives the basket additional protection and also absorb some of the ice melt water on the way. Such baskets are generally used for transporting iced fish by bicycles, hand carts or even as head loads to nearby places.

Drawbacks of Baskets

Baskets have no adequate mechanical strength and so they get deformed under stacking loads thereby transferring compressive loads to the fish which get crushed. Sharp edges cause bruises and cuts on the fish bringing about easy spoilage. They cannot be reused as they cannot be cleaned properly, absorb water and slime and harbour heavy loads of bacteria. But still the baskets are very much in the field because they are cheap and easily available. The cost of packing fish in baskets including palmirah leaf mats/gunny/harhar etc. but excluding cost of ice has been estimated to be around 50 p./kg on an average which is insignificant.

Deal Wood/Plywood Boxes

Second hand deal wood/plywood boxes are generally used in the western parts of the country for transport of fish especially for long distances, by wholesalers and commission agents. If needed the fish is reiced in the boxes enroute. Generally these boxes are used again either by bringing back or for sending iced fish from the wholesale to retail markets. These boxes are also given gunny lining from outside just as in the case of baskets. As these are second hand boxes (tea chests); they are not very much expensive though costlier than baskets. The capacity of the boxes range from 20 to 120 kg. As they are made of wood, a non-conductor of heat, they preserve ice for longer time than the baskets.

During the past decade in India, there is almost a packaging revolution, with the availability of variety of packaging materials, thus generating better packaging consciousness in other producer/food industries. But unfortunately such a realisation is not forthcoming in the fisheries sector, and packaging techniques for domestic trade continues to be on traditonal lines with their inherent drawbacks and limitations. This is probably due to the wrong notion that introduction of any new material, would further escalate the cost of fish. First and foremost need of the hour is to educate the industry on modern packaging methods and right handling procedures and demonstrate to them that packaging could be cost effective.

In the studies carried out by Central Institute of Fisheries Technology, Cochin (CIFT), on the quality of fish and prawns landed at Cochin Fisheries Harbour, only 28 per cent of samples scored excellent rating, 43.8 per cent very good, 20.9 per cent fair to good and 7 per cent as unacceptable. A similar survey carried out on the quality of fish in the retail markets of Bombay, has revealed that only 77.3 per cent of samples were considered as of acceptable quality based on organoleptic evaluation, the most authentic subjective testing of quality, from the consumer's point of view. It is an indication that much of the spoilage is occurring in the transit, either due to unhygienic handling or bad packaging. Even reducing the spoilage by mere 5 per cent would mean saving of Rs.2 million to the nation.

The first development work on the improvement of efficiency of bamboo baskets was undertaken at CIFT, in early 60's, by providing additional linings of polythene and gunny or water resistant kraft paper, thereby enhancing the shelf life of iced fish by 50 to 80 per cent.

The second hand tea chests commonly used in Veraval region of Gujarat, were provided with 2.5 cm thick foamed polystyrene (in polythene sleeving) slabs inside, to improve their insulation value. These containers were found to be extremely beneficial for transport of fish over long distances upto 60 hours' duration. In a comprehensive study undertaken by ICAR under All India Coordinated Research Project on Transportation of Fresh Fish, the various technological problems associated with transport of iced and frozen fish within the country, quality assessment of fish transported by various modes of containers in different regions of the country, thermal efficiencies of the existing and modified containers, amenability of various types of fish in round/filleted form for long distance transportation in iced or frozen state, economics of packaging and transportation systems, etc. and far reaching recommendations were made on the standard to be adopted for handling fish and packing procedures for short and long distance transportation of fish. It was recommended for short distance transportation of iced fresh fish involving of journey less than 16 hours' duration, non-returnable, cheap containers may be used and for distances involving duration upto 16 hours and beyond 16 hours insulated plywood boxes with 25mm thick foamed polystyrene may be used. The ratio of ice to fish recommended is 1:1. For long distance transport, packing the fish in the frozen state (at -18°C) in insulated plywood boxes was suggested so that at the receiving end they are received in thawed condition (below 5°C).

An ideal container for fish packaging, in a tropical country like ours, where the transportation is done under high ambients, from physical point of view, should possess a high net volume to surface area ratio, high insulation value to minimise direct heat losses, and have smooth interiors; economically cheap in relation to their life span, hygienic so as not to be source of contamination by itself, and rigid to withstand handling and transportation hazards. It should be easily stackable and compatible with the mode of transport and storage. In case of reusable container, it should preferably be of collapsible type, to reduce the freight charges of empties. Such an ideal container is difficult to develop, nevertheless a compromise design can be struck with experience. A recent development at CIFT in this direction is the development of an insulated corrugated plastic container which is lightest of all packages available in the country for iced fish transport. A package for holding 30 kg of iced fish weighs less than 2 kg and keeps chilled fish fresh for 60 hours. It is reusable for 5 trips and being of collapsible design and light weight, return of empties is very much cheaper.

Packaging and Transportation Costs

Based on current pricing system of fish, which involves cost of packaging, transport, labour charges and profit margins at various stages of distribution, the cost components of icing, transportation and packaging should constitute a maximum 2.5 per cent to 4 per cent; 2 to 6 per cent and 0.3 to 0.5 per cent respectively of value of fish. Based on these considerations, the most suitable container and ice fish ratio could be worked for a mode of transport and distance. In a tropical country, icing cost rather than the cost of container decides the final cost of fish. Icing costs can be reduced by using efficient container suiting the transit time. A mathematical formula on the expenditures involved in transportation of fish has been evolved at CIFT, taking into consideration the capacity and the cost of container, ice fish ratio (freezing cost in case of frozen fish transport), cost of ice, handling and transportation charges, and so on.

Organisational and Socio-economic Factors

Socio-economic and organisational aspects play very important role in the transport and marketing of fresh fish. The fish landed by fishermen changes hand 2 to 8 times before it actually reaches the end user or consumer. The fish passes through collectors, small merchants, wholesalers, commission agents, auctioners, retailers, etc.

and there is no overall control on the consignments by any authority. There is no organised trade in fresh fish though there are a few big merchants in each centre/area. Under these circumstances it is very difficult to introduce innovations as the cost of innovations has to be born by various people. So if innovations are to be introduced and modernisation is to be brought into the fresh fish transport it is necessary to organise the fresh fish trade. Only an organised industry will be able to invest more for quality and also get better returns by marketing. In the absence of well knit organisation it will be impracticable to use better containers and get back the containers for reuse. Therefore, to modernise the fresh fish transport and marketing, it is essential to have good organisational set-up which will have control over procurement, packing, transport, distribution, etc. Only such organisation can introduce innovations and make profits.

ANNEXURE

Marketing and Distribution of Fish

(a) *Fish landings in India (1989)*

Marine fish	2.25 million tonnes
Inland fish	1.40 million tonnes

(b) *Disposition of fish catch*

Marketing fresh and in edible form	70.8%
Drying/curing	22%
Reduction	5.4%
Miscellaneous purposes	1.8%

(c)

Per capita consumption of fish	4 kg
Percentage increase in consumption	3.5% per year
Consumption of urban and metropolitan cities	45-70%
Consumption of rural areas	30-55%

(d) *Physical flow of fish*

1. Near landing centres	50%
2. Within 200 km distance	45%
3. Beyond 200 km distance	5%

(e) *Transportation of fish within the states*

(a) By road	80%
(b) By rail	20%

Interstate distribution

a) By road	45%
b) By rail	55%

(f) *Storage life and packaging costs of iced fish*

Container	Storage life in hours	Cost of packaging per kg of fish (Rs.)
1. Bamboo basket	11-12	0.25-0.35
2. Bamboo basket lined with polythene and gunny	21-21.5	0.35-0.75
3. Plywood box	14-16	0.50-1.00
4. Plywood box lined inside with 25mm foamed polystyrene	55-60	1.00-1.50

5.	Corrugated plastic container with 25mm foamed polystyrene	55-60	1.50-2.50
(g)	*Freezing cost of fish*	Rs. 2/kg	
	Freezing, packaging, storage and transportation (200 km)	Rs. 5.75/kg of fish	
(h)	*Transportation cost of iced* fish (per kg)		
	By rail		
	Cochin–Bombay	Rs. 3.30	
	Cochin–New Delhi	Rs. 4.80	
	By air		
	Cochin–Bombay	Rs. 8.65	
	Cochin–New Delhi	Rs. 16.00	
	By air (taking into consideration 50% concession on freight rate)		
	Cochin–Bombay	Rs. 4.45	
	Cochin–New Delhi	Rs. 8.15	

THIRTEEN

PACKAGING OF FRESH AND LIVE FISH

C.V.N. RAO

For stabilising the price line and to have even distribution, transportation of any fresh and processed food in space and time is important. Fresh fish is one of the most perishable food stuffs by nature and requires careful handling right from the time it is landed. Functional packaging of fish ensures its delivery to the consumers in prime condition and protects against external stresses. Nearly 70 per cent of marine fish and almost entire quantity of inland fish are consumed in fresh condition. Generally people would like to consume fresh rather than processed fish and this percentage of consumption is likely to go up with improvements in the standard of living. In the studies conducted by CIFT on the quality of fish, at Cochin Fisheries Harbour and retail markets of Bombay, only about 75 per cent of fish can be rated as acceptable quality. Even reducing the spoilage by 5 per cent, would mean saving of Rs.2 million to the Nation. The fish is transported both by rail and road to the interior markets. Fifty per cent of the fish catches are generally consumed within 40 kms distance and the rest is transported within and outside the state, transit times ranging from 4 to 70 hours. The major consuming centres are the metropolitan cities. The packaging of fish is done in traditional containers like bamboo baskets lined with sal leaves and gunny, second hand plywood/wooden boxes etc. Temperature is the most important factor responsible for the rapid deterioration of the quality of fresh fish, especially in tropical climates. Icing the fish is the widely accepted method of chilling the fish as it is economical and readily available. But in commerce, the method of icing is far from adequate, resulting in high temperatures upto 13 to 18°C at various stages of distribution and destinations.

In warm climates, ice does not last longer and every effort should be made to conserve the ice used by employing adequate insulation to the containers. The rate of melting of ice depends on the type of insulation, ambient temperature and the geometry of the container.

Lupin and Boeri have developed simple procedures to calculate the fish to ice ratio and to measure the thermal efficiencies of fish containers based on practical considerations.

A fish container has a definite volume (V_c) and the quantitites of fish and ice it can hold depends on their ratio (n) and the specific volumes of fish (ν_f) and ice (ν_i) (whether it is in flakes, chips or snow) and mathematically written as

$$V_i = M_i (\nu_i + \nu_f \times n) \tag{1}$$

where M_i is the initial quantity of ice used

Normally when the fish is caught its temperature will be at ambient and it should be brought near to 0°C and has to be maintained at this temperature throughout the period from packaging until the point of sale. Thus sufficient quantity of ice has to be added to the fish to chill it to 0°C and to counter the heat gains from the surroundings through the container surfaces into the fish during the storage period. The fish and ice are packed in alternate layers and thickness of which should not exceed 10 cms, to facilitate rapid chilling and to maintain uniform temperatures throughout. Extra amount of ice is needed at vulnerable places where there are more exposures to surroundings such as top and sides of the container.

Ice necessary to cool the fish to 0°C

$$= \frac{(C_f T_f)}{\lambda} M_f \tag{2}$$

where C_f is the specific heat capacity of fish

T_f = Temperature of fish
λ = Latent heat of fusion of ice (usually taken as 80 kcal/kg)
M_f = Mass of fish

C_f varies from fish to fish depending on its fat, solids and water contents and it can be calculated according to equation suggested by Charm:

$$C_t = 0.5X_t + 0.3X_s + 1.0X_m \tag{3}$$

where

X_f = mass fraction of fat
X_s = mass fraction of solids
X_m = mass fraction of water

Ice losses due to heat leakages into the container can be computed by the formula

$$\text{Ice losses} = K.\,T_e.\,t \tag{4}$$

where K = is the specific melting rate of ice in the container in kg/hour/°C
T_e = External average temperature
t = Storage period (hours)

The mass of ice in a container holding fish and ice will be–

$$M(t) = M_i - \frac{(C_f\,T_f)}{\lambda} M_f - K.\,T_e.\,t \tag{5}$$

Substituting (1) in the above

$$M(t) = \frac{V_c}{(\upsilon_i + \upsilon_f n)}\left\{1 - \frac{C_f T_f}{\lambda} n\right\} - K.T_e.t \tag{6}$$

To determine how long ice will last in container we take $M(t) = 0$

$$t_{max} = \frac{V_c}{K.T_e.(\upsilon_i + \upsilon_f.n)}\left\{1 - \frac{C_f.T_f.n}{\lambda}\right\} \tag{7}$$

t_{max} will vary with ratios of ice and fish and is 0 when packed with fish alone and no ice, and maximum when filled with ice alone

If the container is filled with ice alone

$$t^{*}_{max} = \frac{V_c}{K.T_e.\upsilon_i} \tag{8}$$

Dividing (7) by (8) we have

$$\dot{n} = \frac{\upsilon_i}{\upsilon_f} \cdot \frac{1 - \frac{t_{max}}{t^{\bullet}_{max}}}{\frac{t_{max}}{t^{\bullet}_{max}} + \frac{\upsilon_i}{\upsilon_f} \cdot \frac{(C_f \cdot T_f)}{\lambda}} \tag{9}$$

This equation gives the ratio of ice to be used for the expected storage irrespective of type of container used, provided $t^{\bullet}_{max}$ is know for it.

$t^{\bullet}_{max}$ can be determined by studying the rate of melting of ice per hour, by filling the container completely with ice, under steady external comparative conditions. In general, when the trial is conducted under ambient temperatures $t^{\bullet}_{max}$ will fluctuate and in such cases, average melting rate of ice is computed for every 2 hours taking the average temperature and it has been found that the practical and theoretical values are within 20 per cent error limits.

Taking a specific case, supposing

V_c = 65, 000 CC
n_i = 1, 700 cm^3/kg
n_f = 1, 300 cm^3/kg
C_f = 0.8
T_f = 30°C
T_e = 30°C (average)
K = 0.125 kg/Day/°C
t_{max} = 3 days

$$t^{\bullet}_{max} = \frac{65000}{1700 \times 0.125 \times 30} = 10.19 \text{ say 10 days}$$

$$n = \frac{1700}{1300} \cdot \frac{1 - \frac{3}{10}}{\frac{3}{10} + \frac{1700}{1300} \times \frac{0.8 \times 30}{80}} = \frac{1.32 \text{ kg of fish}}{\text{kg of ice}}$$

i.e if the above container takes 10 days for melting of ice when filled completely and for a storage period of 3 days the ratio of fish to ice has to be maintained at 1.32:1. Icing cost of fish per trip of the container can be estimated, by knowing the cost of the container and its expected life span and the cost of ice.

Suppose the cost of container is Rs.100 and can be used for *N* times and the cost of ice is 50 p./kg

$$\text{Cost of ice/kg of transported is} = \left(\upsilon_f + \frac{\upsilon_i}{n}\right)\frac{\text{Cost of container}}{V_c . N}$$

(inclusive of cost of container)

$$+ \frac{1}{n} \text{ cost of ice}$$

$$= \left(1300 + \frac{1700}{1.32}\right)\frac{100}{65000 \times 10}$$

$$+ \frac{1}{1.32} \times 0.5$$

$$= 78 \text{ ps/kg.}$$

The formula can be further modified taking into account cost of wages and transportation costs. CIFT has developed a formula for cost of transportation of fish -

$$a\left[\frac{C}{K} + p + f\left(1 + \frac{W}{K}\right) + \frac{C}{K} + f\left(1 + \frac{W}{k}\right)\right] \quad (10)$$

where C, K, W are the cost, capacity, empty weight of the container and p, a, f are the cost of ice/kg, quantity of ice per kg of fish and freight charges per kg of consignment respectively

or average expenditure $T = a\ (p + m)$

$$\text{where } m = \frac{C}{K} + f\left(1 + \frac{W}{K}\right) \quad (11)$$

Similarly the thermal efficiencies of the containers can be compared by determining ice melting rates under steady conditions of temperature

$$q = AU\,(T_i - T_e)$$

where A = External surface area of the container (m^2)

U = Overall heat transfer coefficient K.cal/day/m^2/°C

T_i = Temperature inside the container (usually 0°C)
T_e = External temperature
q = heat transferred to the container from the ambient

This heat will be counter-balanced by the heat resulting from the melting of ice which is $\lambda.\frac{dM_i}{dt}$

where *Mi* Mass of ice in kg
t time period (days)
Under steady state of heat transfer conditions

$$\frac{d\,M_i}{dt} = \frac{AU}{\lambda}(T_i - T_e) \tag{12}$$

$$\text{Integrating} \int_{M_i^o}^{M_i} d\,M_i = -\frac{AU}{\lambda}(T_e - T_i) \int_o^t dt \tag{13}$$

where M_i° is initial mass of ice in kg

$$M_i = M_i^o - \left[\frac{AU}{\lambda}(T_e - T_i)\right] t \tag{14}$$

or $M_i\ M_i^o - K.t$

where K is the expression in brackets showing ice rate melting index (Rate of ice melted per day).

$$K = \frac{AU}{\lambda} T_3 - \frac{AU}{\lambda} T_i$$

when $T_i = 0$

$$K = \frac{AU}{\lambda} T_3 = K'T_e$$

where $K' = \frac{AU}{\lambda}$

Equation (13) can be written as

$$U = \frac{\lambda(M_i^o - M_i)}{A \int_o^t (T_e - T_i)\, dt}$$

The efficiencies of different containers can thus be evaluated by studying the ice melting constants, under steady state of heat transfer conditions.

In practice, the external temperature varies and all the sides of box are not exposed to the same environmental condition. Nevertheless *U* value is obtained by studying the melting rates of ice over small periods of time well within 20 per cent errors of the theoretical value. *U* value of containers, by determining ice melting rates can be compared.

From physical point of view, high net volume to area ratio is desirable. The containers should be from light packaging materials and should be economical if they are to be used repeatedly. Hygienic factor is important and they should not be a source of contamination and should possess smooth interiors not to injure the fish.

Packaging of Live Fish

In the recent years, transportation of live fish and shell fish is becoming an important activity of the fish industry. With the development of aquaculture, transport of cultured live fish fry, fingerlings and post larve by road, water and air from hatcheries to nearby farms and across the continents is on the increase. Trade in exports of ornamental aquarium fish is a multimillion dollar business. The success for all of which depends on effective packaging techniques and careful handling practices prior to and during shipment with minimum mortality. The important factors to be considered in the shipment of live fish are –

(a) conditioning for a period of time before packing
(b) maintenance of low temperature and high humidity during storage and transit
(c) maintenance of natural environmental conditions
(d) careful handling to avoid stress and injury to fish
(e) stocking density
(f) replenishment of air with oxygen and reduction in accumulation of toxic wastes and controlling acidity of water medium with suitable buffers.

As the packing density is directly proportional to oxygen consumption, this point should be borne in mind, such that there is a minimum mortality during the normal transit time of 3 to 4 days. Conditioning the fish to the environment prior to shipment, lowering of temperature of water and addition of permissible and correct dosage of anaesthetics, reduce their metabolic activity and thus their consumption of oxygen. As the accumulation of carbon dioxide, ammonia interfere with the uptake of oxygen, chemicals such as activated charcoal, clinoptilolites may be added to the water medium to absorb the metabolic wastes. The acidity of the water may be controlled by adding suitable buffers. Healthy fish, good quality of water, its temperature, packing density and proper handling causing least stress and injury to fish are of paramount importance (Fig. 13.1).

Ornamental aquarium fish (2 or 3 nos) after conditioning for a week are packed in a polythene bag (thickness not less than 0.1mm) filled to 1/3 of its volume with sea water containing activated charcoal and flushed with oxygen, and top is twisted, folded and sealed with an elastic band. This may be again placed in another poly bag and sealed as above. The bags are then placed in one or two layers in styrofoam box and finally in an outer corrugated fibre board box and sealed with gummed paper tape. The box should be clearly marked with labels viz. orientation (this sideup), live animals, perishable and other cargo identification marks. The gross weight of the package should be limited to 20 kgs. Fry, fingerlings and post larve may also be similarly packed in oxygenated poly bags, ensuring their stocking density in relation to their size and transit period.

Bulk water transportation of live fish is carried out in live well boats fitted with closed or open circulating pumps and aeration facilities and filters to reduce contamination.

Molluscan shell-fish like clams, mussels and oysters and crustaceans like shrimps, lobsters, crabs are transported at low temperatures and high humidity conditions. Live mussles having thin shells susceptible to easy damage are to be handled with care. They are harvested in clusters to minimise the water loss, and their byssus glands are kept intact to extend their shelf-life. Newzealand green mussels are prechilled in well drained fish cases with a layer of sacking or stockinette place over them and covered with ice (not in direct contact with mussels) to maintain 2 to 4°C. Ten kgs lots are packed in sealed poly bags and are further packed in polystyrene box filled with flake ice and finally sealed with adhesive closure tape.

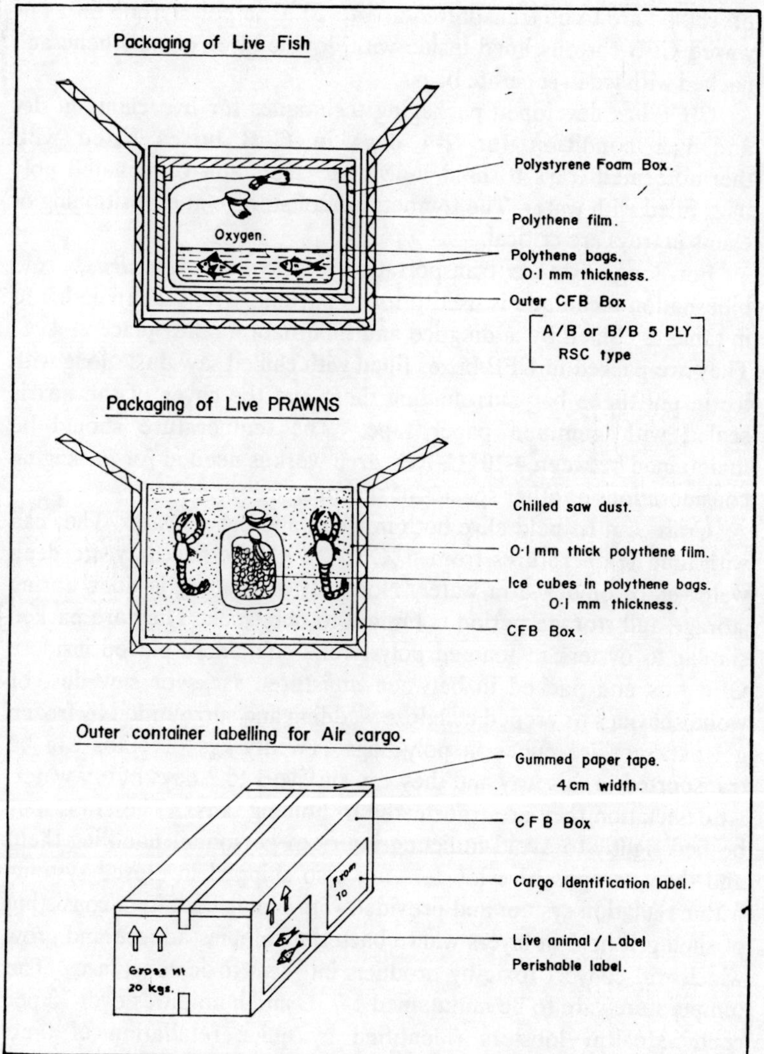

FIG. 13.1: Packaging of live fish, live prawn and outer container labelling for air cargo

Healthy oysters remain closed or shut immediately on tapping. They are to be transported with their cupped half of shells downwards to retain their moisture. Live lobsters which are prechilled are to be transported at 1 to 10°C in polystyrene boxes or waxed CFB cartons lined inside with double layer of polythene and packed with ice in separate bags.

CIFT has developed packaging techniques for live clams in dry and wet condition for 2-4 days in CFB boxes fitted with thermoformed trays to hold individual clams and oxygenated poly bags filled with water. The temperature of storage and positioning of clams in trays are critical.

For long distance transportation of *Penaeus japonicus*, cold hibernation technique is used prior to packing. The shrimp gathered in tanks is chilled by adding ice and hibernation takes place at 4°C. They are packed in CFB boxes filled with chilled saw dust along with ice in polythene bag surrounding them and the cover of the box is sealed with gummed paper tape. The temperature should be maintained between 4-10°C. Research work is needed for packaging considerations of other species of shrimps.

Crabs can be held alive both in water and out of water. They can withstand temperatures from 5°C to 27°C whether they are deep water crabs or of warm water. Normally no feeding is done during storage and storage period is limited to one week. They are packed similar to oysters in foamed polystyrene containers placed inside a CFB box and packed in between moistured sacks or saw dust or wood shavings or creped cellulose wadding and surrounded by frozen gel packs or ice cubes in poly bags. Twenty kgs of crabs can be transported in this way and they can survive 1 to 2 days out of water. At destination they are transferred to holding tanks. The crabs may be tied tightly to avoid inflicting injury to personnel handling them and their escape. Live lobsters are also shipped in closed systems with circulation system and provided with biological filters consisting of shell grit held in layers where bacterial colonies adhere and grow which will convert toxic by products into less toxic substances. The temperatures are to be maintained 1-7°C and humidities over 70 per cent. Healthy lobsters (identified by quick retaliation of their antennae in response to a prod) are to be used. Lobsters are prechilled to 4°C for 12 hours and packed in polystyrene boxes laid with ice pads and impregnated with silicon to absorb melt water. Similar to packing of crabs, metal containers are also used for large scale transportation of lobsters.

Concurrent with the rise in live fish trade IATA, Oriental Air Lines have developed regulations for live shipment packaging standards and specifications of packaging materials, packing methods and labelling instructions.

REFERENCES

Boeri, R.L., et al. 1985: *Int. Inst. of Refrg.* Vol. 8, No. 2, pp.97-101.

F.A.O., *Ibid.*, FII:FTA/11:15P.

Lupin, H.M., 1985: F.A.O. Expert Consultation on Fish Technology in Africa, Lusaka Zambia, 21-25 January.

OAA Packaging Standard for wet shipments.

Richards, P.N., Rajadurai, 1989: *Infofish International* 3, pp.33-37.

Srinivasa Gopal; T.K., Rao C.V.N., Perigreen P.A. and Govindan T.K., 1985: Fishery Technology, 22(1), 48-51.

Warwick, J.C., 1985: *Infofish International* 3, pp.33-36.

FOURTEEN

PACKAGE DESIGN FOR EXPORTS

C.V.N. RAO

Package designing is an unique technological philosophy meeting the various requirements in the overall distribution chain of the manufactured or processed item. Within this definition several functions can be identified – protection and preservation during transit, handling and storage, marketing strategies, rules and regulations, etc. Thus the importance of packaging should be reckoned at the early planning stages of production and marketing and should not be treated lightly or in isolation. Product and package are inseparable like Siamese Twins, as the product is judged ultimately by the package. No body likes a shabbily designed packaged product, whatever be its quality. It is quite clear that the best possible packaging materials meeting the functional needs of the product and aesthetic needs of the buyer should be used. The importance of packaging has been well realised by the advanced nations and fortunately in the recent past. Thanks to the availability of various new packaging materials, India is catching up with this technology. Though development of new packaging techniques has helped the manufacturer in reducing expenses for circulation but this has also brought important social problems like disposal of waste packing materials after use.

However well versed one is in Packaging Engineering, designing an appropriate packaging is a difficult task. Development of good package design requires considerations of product characteristics, circulation route, consumer needs and finally thorough package testing. Over packaging not only increases the cost but creates waste disposal problem and here, the ingenuity of Packaging Engineer comes in availing the existing facilities at minimal overall cost.

Basically, packaging has twin objectives to perform, preservation and protection – preservation of the inherent characteristics of the product and protection against climatic vagaries and hazards encountered in handling, storage and transit such that it arrives at the destination in an acceptable condition to the end user. Goods damaged in transit will neither be sold nor displayed.

Two distinctions have to be made in the type of packaging – (i) consumer packaging and (ii) transit packaging, the former contains the product and preserves the inherent quality of the product until it is sold e.g. tin-plate container, glass bottle, paper board carton, flexible pouch, etc. Packages or the packaging materials are to be selected in accordance with product characteristics. Product characteristics relevant to packaging are –

1. Physical state (weight, volume, stability, finish)
2. Physiochemical effects – Moisture, oxygen, light, temperature, mould, bacteria, fungus, chemical reactions, etc.

Packaging materials are selected to suit the nature of protection needed, its anticipated shelf life, and their compatibility with the product.

Other considertions of the consumer packaging are:

(i) Graphic design and configuration;
(ii) Identification – Brand name of the product;
(iii) Utility – Convenience, easy to open, use or inspection etc.;
(iv) Production – Compatible with the manufacturing process;
(v) Marketing – Moderate number of contents, handy size of package, attractive display, pilfer proof;
(vi) Disposability – To minimise environmental pollution; and
(vii) Economy – In accordance with sale price.

Shipment packages are the external packages containing the unit containers viz. corrugated fibre board boxes, wooden boxes, gunny bags, barrels. These transit packages offer protection against handling and transit hazards. The following points need consideration in designing the transport container.

1. Protection – Against transport conditions

2. Handling	–	Rationalisation of the package size for handling in transit and storage
3. Shipping	–	Conditions of shipping rules, regulations, freight, tariffs, journey hazards.
4. Manufacturing	–	To suit in plant packaging line
5. Functional utility	–	Convenience for inspection staff, handling labour, carrier space.
6. Identification	–	International markings on package
7. Disposability	–	To avoid public hazards and pollution
8. Economy	–	Packaging costs.

Packages are to be designed to withstand journey hazards like –

1. Drops
2. Vibrations
3. Impact
4 Compression
5. Rolling
6. Environmental

Packages can be evaluated in the laboratory for their resistance against these and thus their design can be modified if required.

When a new product is exported for the first time, it is advisable to get the complete information on the legislative and packaging requirements from the buyer. If not available, proceed systematically, bearing in mind especially the following –

(i) Quality of package in confirmity with the product creating right impression as a quality product of India

(ii) Language – not necessarily English

(iii) Convenience – ease of handling storage, display, identification

(iv) Ecology – package easily disposable or recyclable

(v) Marking – International code for quick identification and handling at least on two adjacent sides bearing name and description of article, Port of entry/destination, handling instructions etc. neatly stencilled.

The main problems facing the Indian Exporter would be lack of information regarding laws, regulations, standards effecting packaging materials in the destination markets which vary from country to country. These regulations are mainly aimed at protecting consumers' health and safety, fair trade practices (protecting the consumer against misleading informations) mandatory and voluntary information about the packed products (i.e. composition of the product), protection of environment. Light weight, non-returnable, biodegradable/easily recycled packages are encouraged.

Package designing now means not only concerned with packaging materials but is treated as a complete system suiting the modern mechanical handling devices like fork lifts, air cargo pallets and freight containers by sea, road and air.

Package regulations can be obtained from Department of Commerce and Trade in the target countries, our Embassies, International Organisations like U.N., I.S.O., Packaging Research Organisations, National Standards Institutes, Industries Associations, and so on.

FIFTEEN

PACKAGING OF FROZEN FISH AND FISHERY PRODUCTS

T.K. SRINIVASA GOPAL

Frozen storage of foods is one of the most satisfactory methods of long term preservation of perishable foods provided proper packaging and handling are followed. Although storage temperature of –30°C is ideal and used in most developed countries, –20+2°C is the commercially practiced storage – temperature for frozen shrimp and fish. Fatty fishes are kept between –20 to –30°C. In spite of low temperature, food materials are never completely frozen during commercial storage and deteriorative physical and chemical changes continue at a rate governed by product characteristics and storage temperatures. A primary objective in the distribution of food is preservation of quality during handling, preparation, storage, transportation and sale. To provide frozen foods in perfect condition during storage and distribution the packages must provide protection against dehydration, oxidation, the effects of light and heat, flavour and odour loss and physical damage. Dehydration can be caused by moisture vapour produced by variations of temperature created within the package, being able to escape through the walls of the package or in effect seals. This moisture loss dehydrates the surfaces of the frozen products and causes desiccation, often referred to as freezer burns. Although the desiccated surface layer can be very thin, it may affect the appearance and ultimate solubility of the proteins. Proper packaging for frozen fish is very essential. The advantages of packaging frozen fish are (OECD, 1970).[1]

1. Prevents drying of the product during low temperature storage.
2. Prevents fatty fish from becoming rancid.

3. Protects the contents against physical damage and prevents contamination during handling.
4. Packaging makes the product convenient to handle.
5. Packaging makes the product attractive and arouses consumer interest.
6. Retards any colour change or loss of flavour resulting from the freezing and cold storage process but not necessarily indicative of poor quality.
7. If required it provides for cooking in the wrapper either for convenience or to reduce cooking smells.
8. It provides with interleaving and with individual wrapping, a product which is easily separated into individual portions and permits (Refer, OECD publication) direct cooking without thawing.
9. It provides for quick thawing in water without leaching.

The packaging used for frozen foods should be of good quality as well as odour and taint free in order to prevent contamination of the product by exposure or handling. Thus the product should be totally enclosed and the container should not be capable of being opened without recognisable damage. It should also protect the product against normal transit and storage hazards and inhibit dehydration by incorporating a moisture vapour barrier. All outer packaging should carry clear product identification and should be coded so that the stock rotation can be carried out. In Europe, bags made of polythene are widely used for the packaging of frozen products. Laminated packs are used for quick frozen products. Whilst many unsupported (single ply) packaging films are available, only polythene films find wide acceptance for the packaging of frozen products. Unmodified films are prone to damage when subjected to impact forces under deep freeze conditions. To overcome this, they usually use a co-polymer material like Ethylene/Vinyl acetate (EVA co-polymers) containing 3 to 8 per cent of vinyl acetate (Keith Jeffs, 1988).[2] Laminated materials are widely used for the packaging of frozen products where improved functional or display properties are required. The structures most commonly employed are Polyester/ Polythene and Nylon/Polythene. Most Polyester/Polythene laminates used for deep freezing packaging are based on 12 micron polyester film. The thickness of the polythene layer will be between 40 to 70 micron. In USA greater amount of fish is sold in the frozen form in the super markets. In recent years frozen batter fish products have been on the increase (Sachrow S. Griffin, 1980).[3] The package used is a polythene, wax or hot melt coated carton with or without a waxed paper overwrap. Waxed coated cartons were the first packages used, but problems were encountered with wax flaking off and with dehydration through the score lines on the package. Polythene coated paper board offers good flexibility and better moisture protection. Frozen fish is also found in overwrapped trays displayed in the frozen fish cabinet. The export of seafoods from India in 1990-91 was worth Rs. 878 crores and nearly 75 to 78 per cent in terms of value of this was accounted for by frozen shrimp and frozen fishes. The bulk of the seafood export takes place in the frozen form and export in the canned form is less than 0.2 per cent. Proper packaging for frozen fish is essential for controlling the detrimental effects of oxygen and desiccation by barring the entry of air and escape of moisture.

Current Packaging

The present method of packaging of frozen shrimp in India comprises of LDPE liner (100 guage) or 60 gauge HM HDPE film (T.K.S. Gopal, et al. 1981)[4], or 60 gauge LLDPE film (T.K.S. Gopal, 1987)[5], a waxed paper board (usually duplex board) and corrugated fibreboard box closed with plastic strapping. The carton may be a one piece, top opening tuck on type. 300 to 400 gm/m^2 board is used for the carton and the wax coating varies from 40-50gm/m^2. Dimensions of the carton vary from packer to packer. There are no ISI specifications for these cartons. Ten numbers of these 2 kg (or 5 lb) cartons are packed in corrugated fibre board boxes. There are ISI specifications for these master cartons (IS. 6715-1972). The cartons are nearly cubical in shape (355mm x 300mm x 285mm). They are waxed, but normally only on inside since waxing of the outside makes it difficult to apply any markings. The vertical edges of the box are sometimes strengthened by cloth tapings. The boxes are at times set up by interlocking the bottom flaps. They are closed with the help of HDPE, Polypropylene or Rayon straps and metal seals.

Problems with the Present Packaging

Two of the common defects reported in the master cartons exported from India are low mechanical strength and tendency to get wet. They are easily weakened by deposit of moisture caused by temperature fluctuations during loading, unloading and other handling stages. As a result of this the master cartons become soggy (MPEDA International Trade Centre, UNCTAD/GAT Report 1979).[6] The other problems associated with present packagings are (K.R.Narasimhan, 1982)[7]:

1. Distortion of the inner carton when filled with water.
2. Interlocked cartons tend to tear at the tags. These result in cartons getting distorted in the plate freezer when height bearers and separating bars are not used.
3. Distortion of the cartons affected their fit in the corrugated fibre board box which in turn get distorted and thereby stock stability is affected.
4. Another source of distortion is the prevalent use of the same size of the carton for both 2 kg and 5 lb net weight packs with 13 per cent more shrimps in the latter packs.
5. The use of near cubical corrugated box leads to instability in stacking.
6. Due to the absence of waxing on the outside of the corrugated boxes, they tend to pick up high levels of moisture from condensation which affect their strength.
7. Loosening of the strapping or sometimes breaking at the seal is noticed.

Criticism of Packaging

Since export of frozen shrimps from India is substantial in volume and is steadily increasing, it may seem fair at first glance to conclude that the quality of the product and its packaging is quite satisfactory. This may be true upto a point but there has been enough criticism of quality of both product and packaging to make any complacency out of place. For instance, there have been complaints from the Japanese buyers about damage in transit apart from dissatisfaction over inconsistency in product quality and variation in count.

Therefore, improvement in packaging is required in many ways and the possibilities are discussed below:

Inner Carton

The different types of cartons systems used for packaging of seafood products in different countries are (Infofish, 1982)[8] :

1. Top opening
2. End opening
3. End loading
4. Tray type

In a top opening carton system, filling is done through the largest area of the package. This facilitates filling of products consisting of larger pieces like whole fish, frozen fish blocks and fish fingers. Commercial systems of this type include Stalox, Klikklok, Sprinter, SKA and Diotite. An example of an end opening carton system is the Expresso carton where bottom and top are closed by heat sealing a membrane to the four outfolded flaps. The carton is polythene coated on the inside, the most often also on the outside. The membranes consist of polythene coated paper of film. The system is a unique one walled construct on and replaces the more costly lined carton with a bag inside. This system is choosen when the product to be filled is free flowing and consequently consists of smaller particles or a fluid for instance fish soup.

The end loading carton system feeds the product from one end into a horizontal glued carton. End flaps are sealed with hotmelt or closed by tuck in flaps. End loading is suitable for products packed in aluminium or carton trays. Typical examples are fish dishes and fish gratings in aluminium trays.

Tray type carton systems consist of a bottom carton tray with four narrow flanges and a separate carton lid heat sealed to the flanges. The bottom and lid are plastic coated either on one side or both. The machine system consists of an erecting machine for setting up the bottom part, a conveyor belt for filling and a lid sealer. This type of packaging is utilised for frozen precooked food that will be thawed and heated in the package and sometimes even eaten out of the package. To stand heating, the board is coated with polypropylene or polyester. Polypropylene has a temperature resistance good enough (140 °C) for microwave and hot air ovens. Commercial tray systems of this type are marketed under the trade names Modul, Traylite and Diotray. Maximum machine capacities are 90/minute.

The inner carton should errect without tearing holding the shrimps and water without distortion, close properly, freeze without distortion and fit the corrugated box in the proper manner. Although in the normal course these cartons are not seen by the ultimate consumers, they should atleast match the cartons from other countries (such as Indonesia and Thailand) in quality. A grammage of not less than 360 gm/m^2 would be desirable and stiffness values of 55 gm in machine direction and 26 gmf in cross direction have been recommended. Good quality solid white or duplex board made from virgin chemical wood pulp and better waxing (not less than 15 gm/m^2 on each side should be used) (Narasimhan, 1982).

A recent survey of the waxed cartons collected from 23 factories surveyed from all over India viz. Tuticorin, Kollam, Kochi, Kozhikode, Veraval, Bombay, Paradeep and Kakinada reveals that 56 per cent of the cartons had bursting strength above 6 kg/cm^2, 78 per cent of the cartons had puncture resistance of 26 beach units. About 91.3 per cent waxed cartons are having cobb value below 46. Wax content varied from 2-13.5 per cent, tensile strength varied from 6 to 9 kgf/1.5 cm width/18 cm length. About 35 per cent of the surveyed samples had a tearing strength in the range of 230-280 gm in the cross direction and 33 per cent of the surveyed sample had tearing strength 179-229 gm in machine direction. The thickness of the carton varied from 0.35 mm to 0.6025 mm (K.P. Antony, et al. 1991).[9]

The following specifications have been suggested by CIFT with respect to the unit carton. It should be made from solid white duplex board by chemical wood pulp and should be coated with wax on both sides (the wax used should be extra refined paraffin wax conforming to IS specification IS: 4654-1968).[10] Low density polythene (20 gsm) can also be used for coating. The dimensions of the unit carton should suit the frozen product of 2 or 2.3 kg (net weight). The style of the carton can be any, the commonly used one being the tuck on type. No standards are specified by ISI at present for these cartons. However, the minimum requirements are (Annon 1991)[11]

Grammage	: 300 gsm
Caliper	: 0.4 $\pm$ 0.02 mm
Wax content	: 10 gsm on each side
Polythene coating	: 20 gsm on each side
Ring stiffness	: 270 N
Bursting strength	: 400 kpa

The ink used for printing the carton should be free from toxic metals like lead and chromium. The carton should have the following details printed on its exterior.

1. Name and address of the exporter

2. Brand name
3. Type of product
4. Net content
5. Size grade

For the purpose of inspection the label indicating the code No. and size grade has to be placed inside the carton. Paper code slip should not be used inside the frozen block as it disintegrates and in the importing country it is taken as filth. 150 gauge polyester tracing sheet is found to be an ideal material to use as a code slip. It is non-porous and it retains the original property after wetting (Srinivasa Gopal et al, 1990).

Inner Wrap

Inner wrap should be sufficient enough to be wrapped, folded and to cover the product completely inside the outer carton. Food grade LDPE or HM-HDPE or LLDPE may be used. The thickness of LDPE should be 100 gauge when used as a wrap, 200 gauge when used as a bag. In case of HM-HDPE or LLDPE the thickness should be 120 gauge when used as a bag and 60 gauge when used as a wrap. Where unit cartons are not used, the polythene bag should contain the necessary marking which are otherwise made on unit cartons. Polythene film should be of food grade conforming to IS: 9845 (1981). Following specifications have been suggested by CIFT for LDPE.

Water vapour transmission rate	:	18 gm/sqm/90% RH/ 24 hrs/37°C
Tensile strength	:	Not less than 120 kg/cm^2 in machine direction 85 kg/cm^2 in crosswise direction
Elongation at break (minimum)	:	100 per cent in machine direction 350 per cent in cross direction

Overall Migration Residue

IS test 40°C for 24 hours	:	60 mg/litre or 10 mg/dm^2
FDA test 21°C for 24 hrs	:	50 mg/litre
Flexibility at low temperature	:	Flexible

Master Carton

The dimensions of carton should help the formation of well knit stack. The carton should withstand high moisture conditions as also drops from say upto one and a half meters without damage and should be free from distortions which would present uniform stacking. Two alternate package designs for the corrugated box have been worked out (C.V.N. Rao and T.K.S. Gopal, 1990).[12] The present corrugated box is a Rectangualr Slotted Container (RSC) conforming to style FEFCO 020 which can hold 10 unit cartons in the fashion (2 X 5), 2 per layer and in 5 layers. The boxes by the new design can hold 12 unit cartons in the fashion 3 X 4 to effect savings in the board area used and thus economising in packaging costs. An added advantage of the new design of the boxes is that they are cuboid in shape, thus facilitating easier handling and better stacking. The style of construction of the first case is same as the currently used (RSC) and the second one is similar to wrap around type, adopting which further cost savings in packaging can be achieved (Fig 15.1).

Consider a specific case of packing 60 Nos. of 2 kg nett, frozen, peeled and deveined shrimp having a volume of 2400 CC and size of the duplex board carton 31cm x 15.5cm x 5cm (length x breadth x height). Details of construction of the currently used master case and those of newly suggested ones are presented in Fig. 15.1. Areas of the corrugated fibre board required for the boxes are as follows:

A. *Present method*

1. Area of board required for one case (5 x 2 fashion to hold 10 unit cartons) – 0.76 sqm.
2. Total area of board required for packing 60 blocks in 10 cases – 4.56 sqm.

B. *Alternative methods suggested*

Type 1

1. Area of board required for one case (3X4 fashion) to hold 12 unit cartons – 0.845 sqm.
2. Total area of board required for packing 60 blocks in 5 cases – 4.225 sqm.

A. CURRENTLY USED MASTER CASE

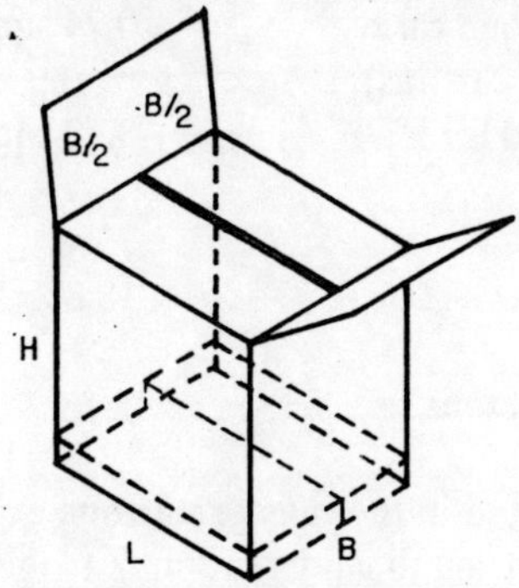

Size of master case.

32 x 32 x 26 cms.

R.S.C Fefco 0201

Arrangement of unit cartons 2 x5

B.1 NEWLY SUGGESTED MASTER CASE

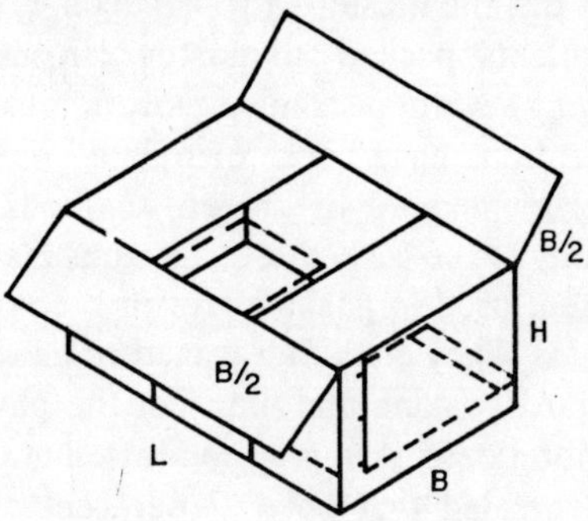

Size of master case

47·5 x 31·5 x 21 cms.

R.S.C FEFCO 0201

Arrangement of unit cartons 3 x 4

B. 2

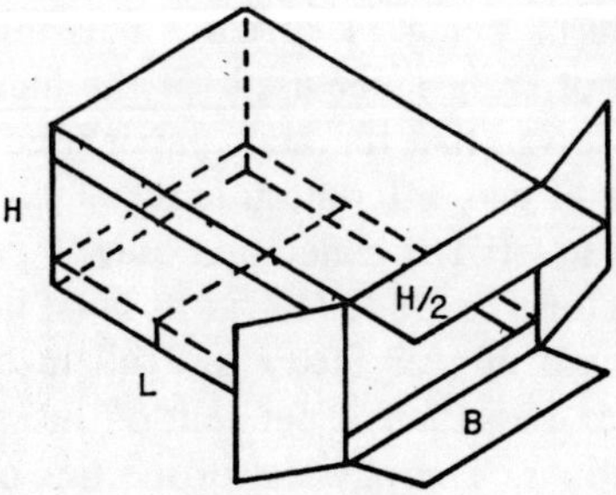

Size of master case

47·5 x 31·5 x 21 cms.

Wrap around type.

Arrangement of unit cartons 3 x

SIZE OF 2 KGS FROZEN SHRIMP (PEELED & DEVEINED) BLOCK

SIZE OF DUPLEX BOARD CARTON 31 x 15·5 x 5 cms. 2400 C.C

FIG 15.1: Master carton

Type II

1. Area of board required for one case (3X4 fashion to hold 12 unit cartons) – 0.74 sqm
2. Total area of board required for packing 60 blocks in 5 cases – 3.70 sqm

% savings of B (1) over (A) – 73%
% savings of B (2) over (A) – 18.8%

Weaknesses Present in Master Cartons

Two of the common defects reported in the master cartons exported from India are low mechanical strength and tendency to get wet. They are easily weakened by deposit of moisture caused by temperature fluctuations during loading, unloading and other handling stages. As a result of this the master cartons become soggy. The gross weight of the contents packed in master cartons lies between 20 kg and 30 kg. Among several packaging materials used in fishery industry, I.S.I. specifications have been formulated only for corrugated fibreboard boxes for export of frozen seafoods and froglegs (IS: 6715, 1972).[13] Many of the 5 ply master cartons made of corrugated fibreboard at present used in packing frozen seafood do not conform to I.S.I specificatios. They are either waxed or unwaxed. There is no uniformity as regards waxing and many of the physical properties of the corrugated fibreboard. A survey conducted at CIFT (K.P. Antony, *et al* 1990)[14] revealed that only 17 per cent of the master cartons conformed to I.S.I. standards with respect to bursting strength, the minimum value of which stipulated for cartons meant for holding 20 to 30 kg material being 14 kg/cm^2. This might be attributed to the poor quality of kraft paper used for the liners and corrugating media. It was observed that the kraft paper used in the fabrication of CFB boxes was of two different grades namely virgin and recycled. A detailed study at CIFT revealed that only 10 per cent of the kraft paper samples conform to grade I as far as burst factor is concerned, 30 per cent in case of tear factor and nil in case of breaking length and cobb value. Less than 60 per cent of the samples conform to grade 2 specifications. The physical properties of kraft paper both virgin and recycled papers exposed to -20°C and 90 per cent RH for three months observed that while both materials have shown decreases in their physical strengths, in case of recycled paper, the changes are pronounced (C.V.N. Rao, et al. 1986).[15] Details are given in Tables 15.1 and 15.2.

TABLE 15.1: Physical properties of kraft paper

Property	Ranges and number of samples (in brackets) falling in them		
	A	B	C
Burst factor	30 and above (2)	30 to 20 (12)	<20 (7)
Breaking length in meters (machine direction)	7000 and above (Nil)	7000 to 4500 (6)	<4500 (15)
Tear factor	120 and above (6)	120 to 75 (12)	<75 (3)
Specific ring crush (cross direction)	75 and above (1)	75 to 50 (4)	<50 (16)
Cobb value (1 minute)	15 and below (Nil)	15 to 20 (7)	>20 (14)

A – Grade 1 as per ISI specification
B – Grade 2 as per ISI specification
C – Others

TABLE 15.2: Physical properties of kraft paper exposed to – 20 °C and 90 per cent RH for 3 months

	Virgin grade			Non-virgin grade (Recycled paper)		
Property	Before exposure	After exposure	% change	Before exposure	After exposure	% change
Grammage (gsm)	123	130	+5.7	119	136	+14.2
Bursting strength (kpa)	335	190	–43.2	230	65	–71.7
Tensile strength kgf/15mm width (machine direction)	8.8	7	–20.5	5.2	3.8	–26.9
Tear strength (g) in cross direction	8	7.5	–6.3	6.2	5.7	–8.0
Ring stiffness (Newtons)	89	69	–22.5	60	42	–30

Indian standards specification for puncture resistance of master cartons is 200 beach units. Only 65 per cent of the cartons conformed to the standards. Most of the cartons (89%) showed low cobb values (below 120). Only 11 per cent of the cartons showed cobb value (30′) more than 120. Waxing alone is not sufficient to reduce the water absorption value. Some percentage of saponifiable matter (usually rosin) and probably other sizing material should also be present in the paper to keep the waterproofness value low.

Improvements in the method of waxing should be effected. Wax coating on both sides is preferred using thermostatically controlled wax coating machine. Alternatively fibreboard boxes which are coated with polythene on one side or both sides could be considered. Shrink packaging/stretch wrapping with polythene can give protection to single/multi carton packs and lend itself to stacking/transportation convenience. The following specifications have been suggested for the master cartons for export.

Grammage of the paper (gm/m^2)	:	140[5]
Bursting strength (kg/cm^2)	:	12
Puncture resistance (Beach units)	:	250
Wax coating (gm/m^2)	:	Waxing on both sides preferred 20 gsm (min) on each side
Compression strength (kg)	:	350 (minimum)
Type of flute	:	B/B (narrow/narrow)
Type of glue	:	Preferably starch based or any other neutral adhesive.

Manufacture Joint

On the outside by staple pins. The width of overlap should not be less than 30mm and fastened by staples not more than 60mm apart in each row and the first and last staples not farther than 25mm from the beginning and the end of the joint respectively. The staples should be centrally located along the overwrap.

Printing

Printing should be in one colour. Each box should have the necessary information legibly and indeligibly marked on the outer surface of the carton.

The exterior of the master carton should have the following information printed on them.

1. Name of the exporter
2. Country of the origin and destination (port)
3. Gross weight, size of the box
4. Name and address of the consignee
5. Transit instructions (for example "perishable" hold at –20°C)
6. Case number
7. Name of product, code number, use bold and clear English capital letters of size 50mm and black waterproof ink for marking. For caution marks use waterproof red ink. Pictorial markings for handling should be used as far as possible along with written instructions in the language of the country of destination which should conform to stipulations of International Standards Organisation.

Strapping

In the Indian frozen shrimp industry the corrugated fibreboard master cartons are reinforced with 12mm wide reprocessed high density polythene/rayon/polypropylene extruded straps. The change over from the conventional steel strapping to synthetic strapping is an important advancement in the reinforcement of the shipping container for frozen prawns. Plastic strappings when maufactured under recommended conditions offer a much higher breaking energy, about twice that of steel. These properties eliminate damages to the product and safe guard against injuries. The fact that India exported 107235 tonnes of frozen shrimp and other frozen fish products in 1991 employing over 5.4 million corrugated fibreboard master cartons reinforced with synthetic strapping materials present some idea about the magnitude and importance of this item of packaging material in the country today in the fishing industry alone. No standards have been prescribed for the requirements of strapping materials to be used in the fishery industry.[16]

The tensile strength of the strapping material must be great enough so that the strapping material will not break when subjected to the sort of load likely to be enountered in practice. In case of polypropylene the fluctuations in the tensile strength and elongation at break (%) at -20°C are comparatively less. Hence polypropylene is more preferred compared to virgin HDPE or recycled HDPE, in which the tensile strength (dry) and elongation at break vary considerably during frozen storage and there are chances that it may give way/may not continue to have a good grip on the master carton during frozen storage, handling and transportation. The following specifications have been suggested.

Material of strap	:	Polypropylene (PP)
Width	:	12mm
Breaking load (kg/cm-width)	:	75 (minimum)
Elongation at break (%)	:	20 (Max.)

Packaging of IQF Products

The frozen blocks of shrimps are sent to international markets as institutional packs and are never sold as consumer packs. The importers thaw out the frozen blocks and pack the shrimps in small retail packs after reprocessing the thawed products. Thus the product losses its Indian identity when sold to the consumer. As the demand for shrimps is ever increasing, the time is ripe for the Indian exporters to add value to their product by exporting in attractive consumer packages and establish a brand image of their own. The market for block frozen shrimps in consumer packs is limited. The growing trend is for IQF shrimps in consumer packs. To gain a wider acceptance of the consumers in the international markets, the shrimps need to be Individually Quick Frozen (IQF) rather than block frozen. The IQF shrimps are highly priced and processed through a complex chain of operations.

One of the recent developments for IQF packaging is the use of laminates since increase foreign exchange revenue can be expected through their export. Europe offers the best opportunity for India to develop consumer pack for IQF shrimps. CIFT has developed flexible packaging material for IQF shrimp based on 12 micron polyester/200 gauge polythene laminate for consumer packs to hold 100 to 200 gm IQF shrimp. Two functional requirements of packing IQF shrimp are worth noting. IQF shrimps are less well protected than the glazed block frozen shrimp against dehydration in storage and oxidative rancidity. Therefore, good quality barrier material is needed in the form of sealed bag as the primary pack for IQF shrimp.

The transit package must have good compression strength since unlike block frozen shrimp packs of IQF shrimp cannot be expected to bear weight without risk of damage to the product. Compression strength should therefore be an items of specification for the transit package. A compression strength of 500 kg has been suggested as a specification which might give reasonable safety.

Other type of packs for IQF shrimps in the Western and the Scandinavian markets are deep drawn plastic pouches. Here vacuum packages of shrimps on roll fed machines with deep drawing of the bottom web are used. The material used is normally PVC of high gauge. This pack may be placed in an outer printed carton.

Labelling and Marketing of IQF Shrimps

The quantity per unit pack varies considerably and is found to be 75gm, 100gm, 200gm for the Scandinavian markets, 100 to 200gm for the UK market and upto 500gm and 1 kg for the French market. The markings required on the consumer pack on IQF shrimps are Type product, Brand name, Country of Origin, Name and address of retailer, Weight, Storage and defrosting instructions, Date of freezing and Storage life. (M.C. Dordi, 1986).[17]

NOTES

1. *Packaging and packaging materials for fish.* Published by Organisation for Economic Cooperation and Development (OECD) (1970), Chapter 4
2. Packaging fishery products in flexible plastic materials and formed trays (1988), by Keith Jeffs, FAO Publication. Published by INFOFISH, Malaysia.
3. *Principles of food packaging.* Sachrow, S., Griffin, R.C., 1980: Ed.2 (1980), AVI Publishing Company, USA
4. High molecular weight high density polythene film for frozen fish packaging. T.K. Srinivasa Gopal et al, 1981: *Journal of Popular Plastics,* Vol.XXVI, No.11, 3-4
5. Use of linear low density polythene film for frozen fish packaging. T.K. Srinivasa Gopal, Jose Joseph and T.K.Govindan, 1987: *Fishery Technology,* Vol. XXIV, No.2, pp 116-118
6. MPEDA – International Trade Centre, UNCTAD/GATT report. The market for Indian Marine Products in Japan, 1979
7. Trends and systems in frozen shrimps. K.R. Narasimhan (1982). Paper presented at the National Seminar on Packing and packaging of marine products held at Hotel President, Bombay during May 1982 organised by MPEDA in collaboration with Indian Institute of Packaging.

8. Packaging trends in frozen foods. Equipment review Karl Axel Bjorkengren 1982, *Infofish Marketing Digest*, May issue, p. 31
9. Survey on the properties of packaging materials for frozen shrimp export. Part II, K.P.Antony, T.K.S. Gopal and P.V. Prabhu (1991). Fishing Chimes, Vol.II, No.6, pp. 62-63.
10. IS — 4654 (1968) Indian Standard Specification for refined paraffin wax
11. Annon (1991) Packages for frozen prawns (shrimp) CIFT report
12. Alternative transport package designs for 2 kg blocks of frozen shrimps. C.V.N. Rao and T.K. Srinivasa Gopal, 1990: *Fishery Technology*, 27 (1), pp. 79-80
13. IS — 6715-1972. Indian Standard Specification for master cartons for export of seafoods and froglegs.
14. Survey on the properties of packaging materials for frozen shrimp export. Part I, K.P.Antony, T.K.S. Gopal and P.V.Prabhu, 1990: *Fishing Chimes*, Vol.10, No.9, pp. 35-37
15. Studies on kraft paper used for liners and corrugating media of shipping containers for frozen shrimp. C.V.N. Rao, T.K.S. Gopal and T.K.Govindan, 1986: *Fishery Technology*, 23 (2), pp. 217-218
16. Alternate code slip for frozen shrimp packaging. T.K.S. Gopal, T.S.G. Iyer, P.V.Prabhu and K.Gopakumar, 1980: *Seafood Export Journal*, Vol.2, pp. 1-3
17. Packaging of shrimps. Mrs. M.C. Dordi, 1986: Packaging of food poducts, Indian Institute of Packaging, pp. 113-120

SIXTEEN

PACKAGING OF DRIED FISH AND DRIED FISH PRODUCTS FOR EXPORT AND INTERNAL MARKETING

K.P. ANTONY

About 20 per cent of the total marine fish catch in India is preserved by drying mostly sun drying. In 1988-89, 4007 tonnes of salted and dried fish were exported. The usual dried fish exported are seer, tuna, perchs, caranx, sprats, anchovies, Bombay duck, etc. The important dried fish production centres in India are Kozhikode, Mangalore, Veraval, Kakinada and Tuticorin. Poor quality dried fish is often produced, as good quality raw fish is utilised for other types of preservation and also sold fresh. Packaging can never improve the quality of the items packed, but can at the most keep the initial product quality intact.

It is estimated that around 25 to 30 per cent of the dried fish produced in India is wasted mainly due to insect attack, rodent attack, microbial attack and fragmentation. The only possible way to minimise this loss is by properly controlling the processing parameters, handling, packaging, storage and distribution. Packaging has a vital role to play in dried fish production and storage.

Packaging has many functions to serve for reducing losses in dried fish production. It is generally seen that the methods of handling and processing employed and the packaging materials used for the dried fishery product leave much to be desired from aesthetic and hygienic points of view. The basic functions of any package may be mentioned as containerisation, enabling the fish product to be handled conveniently as a single unit. Hazards in handling and distribution shall be minimised. Besides, the packaging should help to store, transport and distribute the product safely. Information on grade, destination and ownership should be well displayed on the container. While fulfilling these functions the package should also assist to minimise the unit cost of the product. The special functions required of a suitable dried fish/product package are inertness, leak proofness, impermeability to oxygen and moisture and translucent. Resistance to mechanical abrasion and puncture is another desired quality. Above all the packaging must be as inexpensive as possible to reduce the escalation of the price of fish.

Commonly available single web films like low density polyethylene or polypropylene are used for dried food products other than dried fish. The high moisture content in dried fish leads to microbial attack when such films or packages lined with such films are used. However, dried fish can be packed in packages if the products are sufficiently dried to a moisture level of 25 per cent or less. When dried fish having 35 per cent moisture content is to be packed, it has to be treated with suitable chemicals to protect them from mold attack and rancidity.

While packing fish either wet or dry certain inherent problems are seen, compared to other food products. Dry fish is usually irregular in shape leading to difficulty in assembling in a neat package. They have sharp spines and projections which may puncture the packaging materials. If the packages are porous they become permeable to insects. Because of the permeable nature of the common packaging material namely jute sack, salted dried fish may absorb moisture and expell it during dry season. For safe and better storage the product should have water activity of less than 0.6. In atmospheres around the coastal belt of India, the Relative Humidity (RH) is usually more than 60 per cent. Consequently the salted dried fish absorbs moisture. This results in microbial infestation and spoilage. Proper chemical treatments are needed to prevent the spoilage.

Packaging of dried fish is a neglected area in marketing. Commonly used package in the countryside is either old news papers or dried leaves. However, bulk packaging materials have become essential for the trade and transport. The bulk packaging materials tried for commercial use in India are (1) Waxed corrugated cartons (2) Dealwood or plywood boxes (3) Bamboo baskets (4) Gunny bags (5) Dried palmirah or coconut palm leaf mats and (6) Multiwall paper sacks.

The merits and demerits of the above packaging materials are given below:

1. *Waxed corrugated cartons*

Merits	*Demerits*
(i) Handy, light, hygienic and presentable	(i) Very delicate, needs careful handling.
	(ii) Not proof against insects, rodents, moisture, breakage
	(iii) Costly

2. *Dealwood or plywood box*

(i) Compact and strong	(i) Comparatively heavier
(ii) Larger quantity can be press packed	(ii) Cost is high
(iii) Handling, transportation and stacking are easy	(iii) Cheap wood is not easily available
(iv) Can be reused	
(v) Protection against breakage	

3. *Bamboo baskets*

Almost same advantages and disadvantages as that of corrugated cartons, except it is cheap.

4. *Gunny bag*

(i) Light, handy, cheap, proof against breakage	(i) Not proof against moisture, insects, pilferage and not hygienic

5. *Dried Palmyrah palm leaves and Coconut palm leaves*

(i) Cheapest of all and readily available in the coastal regions of India	(i) Not hygienic, not proof against moisture and insects and easily attacked by rodents. Packing is laborious and does not give a good appearance.

6. *Multiwall paper sacks lined inside with 300 gauge LDPE*

(i) Hygienic, presentable and can be printed	(i) Costly, polythylene lining may break at the stitch, during handling and all the defects of gunny bags may be applicable here also.

Indian Standards Specifications do not prescribe any particular packaging material for export of dried fish, but the Export Inspection Rules (1969) provide that "The dried shark fin and dried fish maws shall be packed in a manner agreed between the exporter and the foreign buyers and in the absence of any such agreement the material shall be packed in sound gunny bags". At present in Tuticorin region dried fish is packed in hundred weight (C wt) packs, (50 kgs) in dried palmirah leaf or dried coconut palm leaf and tied with a coir rope, lined outside with a jute cloth and stitched with a single jute twine. The dimensions of the packages are approximately 61X35X51 cms. The net weight of the packaging comes to 2 kg and costs Rs.10. This kind of package is found to be inadequate often in hostile weather conditions. These conventional packagings are also permeable to oxygen and moisture leading to rancidity and rehydration. Such packaging may also result in heavy product and financial loss also rendering the product unfit for human consumption.

Improvements in Commercial Retail Packing of Salted Dried Fish

Usually salted dried fish, shell-on dried prawn and dried prawn pulp are bulk packed in packages described earlier. Bulk packages render handling of the material and maintenance of proper hygienic conditions in retail distribution difficult. The shelf-life of salted dried fish and its moisture content are directly related. They can be commercially packed in 300 gauge low density polythene for 120 days without much damage. If the moisture content is above 25 per cent this product has to be treated with 0.1 per cent calcium propionate (w/w) and then packed and sealed. Such products in sealed condition may remain in good condition for upto 180 days in the ambient conditions (RH 62 to 98 per cent and temperature 25°C to 35°C). The basic advantages of the low density polyethylene are, clarity, low water vapour transmission rate, good bursting and tearing strength and heat sealability. One major disadvantage of polyethylene film is its high gas transmission rate. Unlike other processed food items consumer packages of high gas transmission rate are not desirable for dried fish products as the smell of products dissipates to the surrounding atmosphere. MXXT/PE laminate manufactured by Travancore Rayons Ltd. has been identified as a suitable packaging material with negligible gas transmission rate suitable for packing dried fish. The laminate is made of 'dry lacquer process' from 150 gauge LDPE and 30 g/sqm. saran coated cellophane. Colour printing is possible on this laminate. Physical properties of the laminate are given below:

Physical properties of MXXT/PE film

1. Substance g/m^2 – 72
2. Bursting strength kg/cm^2 – 3
3. Water vapour transmission rate g/m^2/24 hrs at 38 °C and 90 per cent R.H. – 6.2
4. Heat seal strength kg/3.5 cm – 2
5. Heat seal temp. °C – 100-115
6. Gas transmission rate – negligible

Shell-on dried prawn and prawn pulp are commercially well accepted if they are packed in the above packages. This type of prawns having only 14.2 per cent moisture content were found to puncture any type film or laminate. Hence, they are primarily packed in duplex cartons of 30X14.5X6 cms and an outer packing is given with the above laminate. The product thus packed remained in good condition upto 250 days without any treatment. Shell-on dried prawns can be packed in MXXT/PE laminate for commercial purpose provided head, tail and legs are removed. They possess the same storage life as the shell-on packed product.

Improvements in Commercial Bulk Packaging Salted of Dried Fish

In jute sacks lined inside with 300 gauge polyethylene, the lining was seen often broken during handling leading to moisture absorption. Further this led to wetting of sack cloth making both the material and sack cloth unhygienic by contamination from the environments often heavily polluted. Breaking of the lining makes insect entry rather easy.

High Density Polythene (HDPE) woven gussetted bags laminated with 100 gauge low density polythene are found very much suitable for dried fish packaging. HDPE is a plastic material which never rots even on wetting unlike the jute cloth. Besides HDPE is highly crystalline and is hard and translucent. It has a high tensile strength, an added advantage. From the hygienic points of view HDPE is impervious to microbial and insect attack. The cost Rs.12 for packing 50 kgs of dried fish compared to the traditional system of packing is expensive. However, this drawback is compensated by its various advantages. Places where HDPE woven sacks are not available, woven polypropylene bags may be used (Fig. 16.1).

Packaging of other Dried Fishery Products

Accelerated Freeze Dried (AFD) prawns have captured good market in recent times, particularly in export to Japan. They are in demand due to their superior quality in spite of higher cost of production. Besides export they are very important for incorporating in army rations and in other emergency foods. AFD fish weigh only one-fifth of fresh fish (edible meat w/w). The moisture content is generally below two per cent. Hence, such dried material has to be packed in inert gas so as to exclude air/oxygen. The packaging material must have low oxygen and water vapour transmission rates in order to protect the material from rancidity and absorption of water. Laminated metal foils are used for packing AFD fish. In some cases, metal containers like tin cans have to be used to protect from shock as the material is very brittle.

A suitable packaging for fish meal, poultry feed, cattle feed incorporating fish meal must be moisture proof, inexpensive and impermeable to oxygen. But these materials at present are stored and transported only in gunny bags. Gunny bags made of jute have all the drawbacks. Gussetted bags made of woven HDPE or polypropylene can be used in this case also.

FIG. 16.1: Fifty kg. capacity HDPE woven sack for bulk packaging of salted and dried fish

SEVENTEEN

VALUE ADDED MARINE PRODUCTS AND THEIR PACKAGING

P.A. PERIGREEN

The fish processing industry in India is mainly export oriented and the major portion of the exports is contributed by block frozen and individually quick frozen shrimps, lobsters, squid and cuttle fish. But in recent years attempts have been made for the diversification of the products for exports. A number of value added marine products both for export and internal markets can be prepared from shrimp, squid, cuttle fish, certain species of fish and minced meat from low priced fishes. Development of suitable packagings for these value added products is also important.

Battered and Breaded Products

Most important class of value added marine products is battered and breaded products. The methods and recipe for the preparation of battered and breaded fish products are given below.

Batter mix

Consists of ingredients which when diluted with water, assist in governing amount of breader pick up as well as imparting flavour. Specific ingredients are used to aid viscosity, texture and adhesion. Normally, a seafood batter will contain a high amount of adhesive starch as base. A special batter mix using native ingredients suitable for the fish products can be formulated using wheat flour, corn flour, sugar, salt, edible gum and small amounts of spices.

Breadings

Japanese style bread crumbs are generally used for this purpose. These bread crumbs are very porous, extremely tender and crisp and availabe in attractive colours. This type of bread crumbs are not commercially produced in India.

The battering and breading are usually done in two stages – first battered product is coated with predust (fine breader), rebattered and coated with Japanese style bread crumbs. The battered and breaded products contain more than 50 per cent fish portion. The battered and breaded fish products are flash fried at 175 to 180°C for 20 to 30 sec. and packed in suitable containers and frozen stored. A number of value added battered and breaded products can be prepared from shrimp, squid, fish fillets, clams, minced meat, and so on.

Prawn products

(a) Battered and breaded peeled prawns
(b) Battered and breaded shrimp – fan tail (butterfly)
(c) Battered and breaded shrimp round-tail on

Squid products

(a) *Squid rings*

Cleaned squid tubes are cut in the form of rings, cooked for 1-2 min. in boiling brine (3%), cooled, battered, breaded and flash fried for 20 sec.

(b) *Stuffed squid*

Prepared from small squid tubes. The tubes are cooked in 3 per cent brine for 5 min. and cooled. The tubes are then filled with stuffing mixture prepared using cooked squid tentacles, potato, fried onion, spices, etc. The stuffed squid is then battered, breaded and flash fried.

Fish Fillets

Skinless fillets of fish are slightly brined and allowed to drain. The drained fillets are dipped in batter and coated with bread crumbs. The battered and breaded fillets are then flash fried at 175 to 180°C for 1 minute.

Clam Products

Clam meat is obtained from depurated clams. The meat is blanched battered, breaded and flash fried.

Minced Fish Products

Minced fish is the flesh separated in a comminuted form from the skin, bones, scales and fins of a wide range of fish species. This minced fish can be used for the preparation of a number of value added products like fish fingers, fish cutlets, fish patties, and so on.

(a) *Fish fingers*

Minced fish is mixed well with one per cent salt and frozen in the form of slabs. The slabs are then sawed into fingers of uniform size (15mm X 15mm X 75mm), and coated with batter and breading mix. The battered and breaded product is flash fried at 175 to 180°C for 20 sec., frozen and packed (The fish fingers can also be prepared from frozen slabs of fish fillets).

(b) *Fish cutlets*

Fish cutlet is prepared from cooked fish mince. The cooked mince is mixed with cooked potato, fried onion, spices, etc. and formed into round shape (40 gm). The formed cutlets are battered, breaded and flash fried.

(c) *Fish patties (burgers)*

Prepared from lean white fish mince. The cooked mince is mixed with cooked potato, mild spices etc. and formed into round shapes. The product is battered, breaded and flash fried.

Fish in Sauce and Fish Salads

These are two important groups of ready-to-serve value added products. Fish fillets, tuna steaks, cuttle fish cubes, squid rings, cooked shrimp and boiled clams are suitable for the preparation of such products and sauces used include lemon butter sauce, myonaise sauce and tomato sauce. The main ingredients in fish salad are cooked fish (35-40%), salad dressing (25-30%), cooked macaroni (15-20%) and small quantities of onion, celery, capsicum, pepper and lime juice. These products are preserved by freezing.

Importance of Proper Packaging

The changes taking place during frozen storage of the above mentioned products are desiccation, discoloration, development of rancidity, etc. Application of proper packaging prevents/retards these changes and enhance shelf-life. Conventional packaging materials like flexible plastic films alone are not suitable for these products as they provide little mechanical protection to the products and as a result the products get damaged or broken during handling and transportation. Hence thermoformed containers or carton packing are commonly used for this purpose.

Thermoformed Containers

Blisters, multicavity trays, thin wall containers, ice-cream cups, etc. are some of the packages which at the moment are getting great attention in Indian markets. These, all together, form a group of containers called thermoformed packaging containers. Thermoformed packagings are produced by the process of thermoforming which is commonly known as vacuum forming. In the process, thermoplastic sheets are heated to make them soft. While in soft condition, these are draped over moulds which give them desired shape. By choosing right materials and right shapes, these containers can be used to pack various products in different fashion.

Thermoformed Trays

The thermoformed trays are produced from plastic sheets which have built in cavities or without cavities. The number, shape and size of cavities are determined by the product to be packed. These trays are very useful for window display of consumer products. Since the shape cavities can be designed to match the contours of the product, the chances of breakage or damage by mutual collision of products is minimised, which is necessary for packaging of fragile and delicate items.

Although at present, the use of these containers in India is limited due to cost factor, their use is increasing steadily, specially for ice creams and dairy products. The process of packing fishery products in thermoformed trays is given in Fig. 17.1.

Material for Thermoformed Packagings

For thermoformed trays, polyvinylchloride (PVC), High Impact Polystyrene (HIP) and High Density Polyethylene (HDPE) are mostly used. The thickness of sheets used varies from 0.25 to 4.0 mm depending upon the weight of the products to be packed. For packing food products, only food grade materials should be used. The properties of PVC and HIP materials are given below.

	PVC	*HIP*
Specific gravity	1.4 to 1.6	1.05 to 1.07
Tensile strength (lb/inch2)	6500	4500-5500
Hardness	D 75 – 85	R 45 – 60
Softening point (°C)	70	85-90
Water absorption (24 h), %	0.1 to 0.4	< 0.25
Impact strength (ft lb/in of Notch)	–	9

(*Source*: Plastics in Packaging)

Advantages

1. Low tooling cost
2. Small quantities can be produced economically
3. Containers with wall thickness as low as 0.1 mm can be produced
4. Being display package, products get high sales appeal

Disadvantages

1. Usually it alone cannot be used as a transport pack
2. High cost of raw material
3. Package wall thickness varies from point to point because of process itself

(Arun Bhargava, 1984)

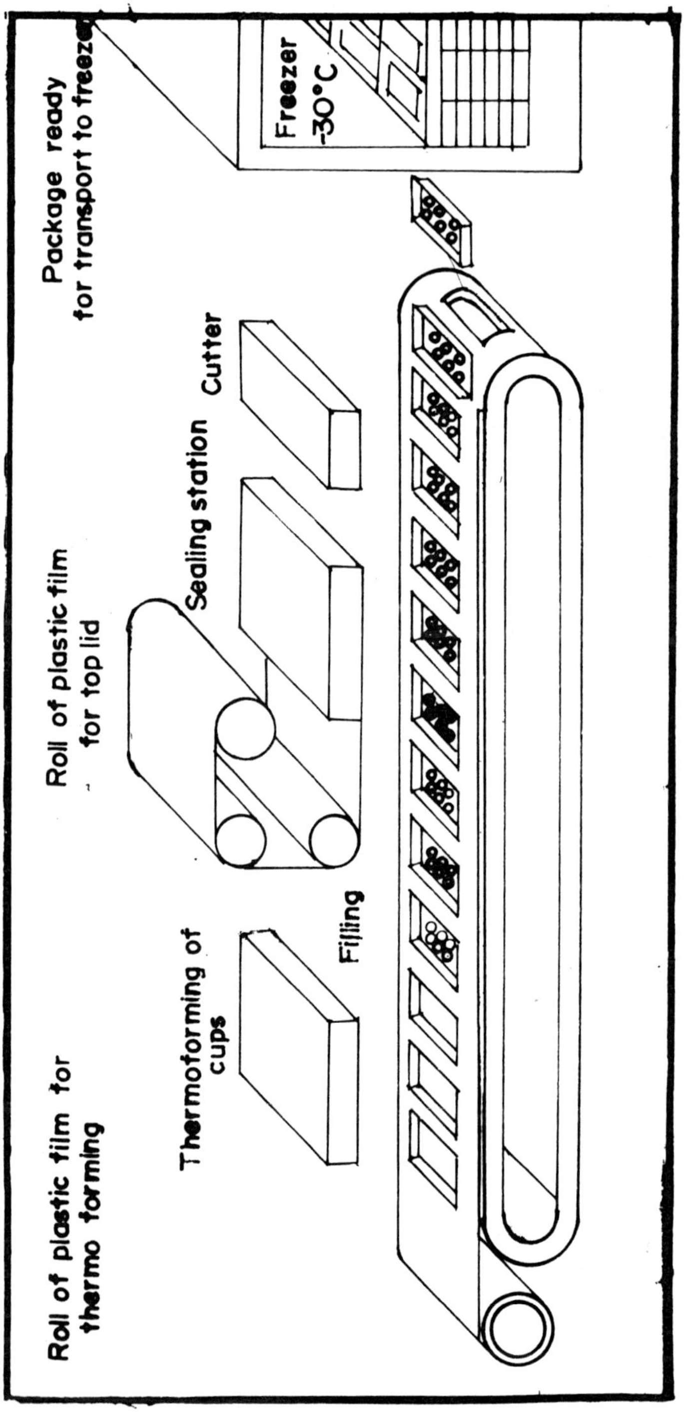

FIG. 17.1: Thermoformed tray packaging
(Courtesy: Infofish Marketing Digest, May 1982)

Packing in Cartons

In this case, the value added fish products are first packed in a flexible container (made of polyester, high density polythene, etc.) and sealed. This is then put in waxed cartons made of duplex board. The outer carton protects the material packed in flexible pouches from mechanical damage. This type of packaging is suitable for packing 250 or 500 gm fish products for retail consumer markets.

Other Materials

Co-extruded sheets of materials with different physical properties are being developed to get economical packs with optimum physical properties. Introduction of Expanded Polyethylene (EP), Expanded Polystyrene (EPS) and thermoformable sheets with high cushioning property is another development. The very low density of EP and EPS allows to produce containers economically.

Conclusion

The thermoformed trays produced from food grade materials are suitable for the packaging of value added fishery products both for internal and export markets. Trays made of materials like PVC, HIP and HDPE are unaffected by low temperature of frozen storage and protects the contents even during prolonged storage. Alternatively, the frozen fishery products like fish fingers, burgers, etc. can be packed first in flexible film and then enclosed in cartons made of waxed duplex board.

REFERENCE

Arun Bhargava (1984) in Plastics in Packaging, p. 258, Indian Institute of Packaging, Bombay.

INDEX